W. B. YEATS

THE TR

A STUDY OF THE LAST POEMS

by

VIVIENNE KOCH

THE JOHNS HOPKINS PRESS

Baltimore 18, Maryland

First published in 1951
by Routledge & Kegan Paul Ltd.
Printed in Great Britain
by Latimer Trend & Co. Ltd. Plymouth

W. B. YEATS:

THE TRAGIC PHASE

If we learn to read poetry properly, the poet never persuades us to believe anything. . . . What we learn from Dante, or the Bhagavad-Gita, or any other religious poetry is what it *feels* like to believe that religion.

T. S. ELIOT

We only begin to live when we conceive life as tragedy.

W. B. YEATS

ACKNOWLEDGEMENTS

Acknowledgements are made to Mrs. W. B. Yeats for permission to reprint thirteen poems from *Last Poems and Plays* by W. B. Yeats (Macmillan & Co., Ltd.).

I am happy to acknowledge the generous assistance of the Rockefeller Foundation for study in England toward a work on modern poetry, of which this book is a part.

I am thankful to Mr. Malcolm Merritt and Mr. Andrew McDermott for compiling the index and for graciously helping with various troublesome matters.

I also wish to thank Miss Elizabeth Drew for the benefit of her reading.

FOREWORD

I have made the following readings of what I consider to be the most interesting and the most difficult of Yeats's *Last Poems* with the end in view of making them more immediately accessible both to readers of his poetry and to those who read poetry but do not know the *Last Poems*. The fact that the *Last Poems* were almost unavailable during the war and post-war years has left a gap of ignorance concerning them even among the many readers of Yeats's earlier work. While his publishers in England have recently released a new edition of the *Last Poems*, as part of the long-awaited and definitive *Collected Poems*, the final proof of which Yeats corrected on his death-bed in 1939, considering the great demand for these poems both in England and the United States, this edition may not at once meet the public need. Partly to alleviate this situation, but more primarily to make the job of continual textual reference (without which I do not believe poetry can be profitably discussed) more convenient for the reader, I have prefaced each of my discussions of a particular poem with the text of that poem as given in the 1940 edition of *Last Poems and Plays* (Macmillan).

My method of reading these poems can be best seen in the readings themselves, and I do not think it useful to recapitulate here the critical values which such a method, of course, implies. There is certainly no longer anything 'new' in this way of reading a poem, and I do not think it is necessarily the only way to read one. But I do think it the best way to read a poem as *poetry*, and not as a number of other things like 'philosophy', 'history', 'sociology', 'ideas', or anything else which poems are sometimes taken to be. It will be seen that my method varies a little from poem to poem, and I hope this will be judged to be the result of necessities set up by the individual poem.

While I do not think we should want to read all poems as I have read these poems of Yeats, I do believe that this approach may suggest one for the reading of other poets as well. The chief things in it are, first, a willingness to let that particular poem take hold of the imagination as if it were—at the moment of scrutiny —the only poem in the world; second, to let only that particular poem and no other source—whether in poetry or in prose—determine, *in so far as is possible*, what its meaning is. This means a trust in the poem, which, if we cannot give it, should make us suspect it as poetry.

But, it will be pointed out, I say in these pages that there is a direction, a 'theme', to these last poems of Yeats. This does not violate the essential empiricism of my method. The fact that each poem must *first* be thought of as an entity, as that thing and no other, does not mean that together a number of poems do not suggest a pattern. The pattern I have found is that these great but troubled poems derive their energy from suffering, describe the process of suffering, and,

8

in the end, celebrate suffering not only as the inevitable condition of living, but as a sign that we truly live. I have indicated that for Yeats this pattern was most observable in the paradox of sex, and that from the configuration and incidents of sexual conduct he was able to construct a field of meaning upon which he drew, in these poems, for subject, language and imagery. While this direction can be seen in all the circumstances surrounding this period in Yeats's life, it is the poems themselves that first evoked it for me, and I have referred to the circumstances only where they had some verifiable and relevant assistance to offer to the poem.

VIVIENNE KOCH

CONTENTS

FOREWORD   *page* 7

INTRODUCTION   13

THE POEMS

GROUP ONE

1. THE WILD OLD WICKED MAN   29

2. AN ACRE OF GRASS   43

GROUP TWO

1. THE STATUES   57

2. A BRONZE HEAD   77

GROUP THREE

1. THE GYRES   91

2. THE MAN AND THE ECHO   113

GROUP FOUR

1. THE THREE BUSHES   123

2. THE LADY'S FIRST SONG   126

3. THE LADY'S SECOND SONG   *page* 126

4. THE LADY'S THIRD SONG   127

5. THE LOVER'S SONG   128

6. THE CHAMBERMAID'S FIRST SONG   128

7. THE CHAMBERMAID'S SECOND SONG   128

CONCLUSION   147

INDEX   149

INTRODUCTION

In this study I wish to consider chiefly two aspects of the poetry of Yeats's last years, that poetry which reached and held to the 'intensity' which he had striven for all his life. I see its prevailing tragic quality as a revelation of Yeats's final bitter vision that the creative conflict in which he centred the dynamics of all cosmic and human relations could not be resolved. In the curious little document called 'Geneological Tree of Revolution' which his recent biographer, Dr. A. Norman Jeffares, appends to his work,[1] Yeats made an outline for a socio-cosmological work which he never wrote. The common philosophical sources of his 'Tree' are Nicholas of Cusa, Kant and Hegel. Two chief branches depending from them are 'Dialectical Materialism (Karl Marx and School)' and 'Italian Philosophy (influenced by Vico)'. Under a fourth heading, 'A Race Philosophy', a title which betrays the naïve character of Yeats's thought, he writes: 'The antinomies cannot be solved.' The antinomies are those he has lumped together under the heads of 'Dialectical Materialism' and 'Italian Philosophy'. The significance of this for readers of his poetry is that for Yeats the antinomical

[1] *W. B. Yeats: Man and Poet*, London, Routledge & Kegan Paul Ltd., 1949.

13

nature of human experience was pervasive whether in the individual, the State, or in the cosmic forces—environment, history, or 'Body of Fate', to use his eccentric terminology—which surround man.[1]

Another feature in the last poems to which I wish to draw attention is intimately related to the first. Indeed, it is a nice question, but one which I will not presume to settle, just which is cause and which is effect. It is that the profound agony of Yeats's conflict ('The antinomies cannot be solved') is at once the source, energy and theme of his last poems. In old age, Yeats became a great poet but he was more than conscious that he had not become a great man. What gives a tragic cast to the work done in his seventies is his own perception of the gap between aspiration and achievement, between the source and the end which is the created object. It was the 'foul rag-and-bone shop of the heart' which he knew to be the raw material of the nobly resolved didacticism of his poetry.

While I do not for a moment wish to direct this study to a biographical reconstruction of Yeats's last years, it is impossible to read these poems without reading the spiritual biography of those years. But, if we do this, we must always remember that we read the poem only incidentally for the biography and primarily for the poetry. Other men have no doubt suffered as Yeats suffered; other men have found in old age no resolution for the multiplicity of choices open to experience. In *Four Quartets* Eliot testifies:

[1] There is little doubt that Yeats's early study of Blake's cosmological poems helped this concept to mature.

14

It was not (to start again) what one had expected.
What was to be the value of the long looked
  forward to,
Long hoped for calm, the autumnal serenity
And the wisdom of age? Had they deceived us
Or deceived themselves, the quiet-voiced elders,
Bequeathing merely a receipt for deceit?

But Eliot discovers for himself a solution which is beyond time, having its locus in mystical experience, and so beyond the exigencies of the specific issues posed by age, itself, as a problem. This is not so with Yeats. His terror is not the terror of a Christian; his suffering does not transcend its source and become the suffering of a saint or a religious. But the suffering itself becomes the great human motive and dynamic of his work. And, at the end, it is the burden of his words as well.

Now the terms in which Yeats expressed this suffering in the last seven or eight years of his life were very largely sexual. One could go further, but it would not add to the poems' value, and say that the cause of his suffering was sexual. The one critic of Yeats who alone has properly tackled this grave and portentous area of his work, Dr. J. Bronowski, is not primarily interested in Yeats's technical achievement but in placing him in a geneological line which connects him with Blake and Swinburne. His argument is this: all Yeats's poetry was dominated by the value of purpose; not just Christian purpose, but any purposive energy. Yeats lost faith in purpose because he lost faith in his own purpose. After *Responsibilities* (1914) Yeats 'sets living against poetry and above it'. This opposition now becomes the theme of Yeats' poems. From about 1929, as suggested in the second Byzantium poem:

'Yeats sees the mystic life as the sexual life. He who had sailed to Byzantium because the sexual world belongs to the young in one another's arms now praises Byzantium because he finds there a spawning and sexual life more exciting than that which he has left. There "Godhead on Godhead in sexual spasm begot Godhead". The love of women has at last come into its own. . . . Everything he writes now is to say this: that the ideal lives because it is sexual. . . . He has made the abstract life more real by making it sexual.'[1]

And, while taking his symbol for this from Blake, he has gone farther because he 'has taken the social beliefs of the nineteenth century into mysticism. He has made the social life the life of the senses alone. . . . He has made the life of the senses the ideal from which poetry takes its worth.'

The conclusion Dr. Bronowski draws from these interesting observations seems to me at once over-simple and over-inclusive. At the end, he says, 'Yeats stands against the line of poets whose ideal was poetry. . . . He is a great poet of living and of the senses. . . . Yeats is a poet great enough to stand against poetry.' Earlier, Dr. Bronowski had made an opposition between poetry and living. Now one sees he is fitting

[1] *The Poet's Defence*, London, Cambridge University Press, 1941.

16

Yeats into an antinomy of his own. But, it is possible even at the start of this inquiry, to say that Dr. Bronowski's is a superfluous antithesis. There is nothing in the identification of the mystical with the sexual experience to preclude the poetic act, which, in the passionate style in which Yeats wanted it, is to temporarily transcend the ordinary modes of experience.

Yeats's biographers have been casual about this. Hone is aware of Bronowski's point, and while he himself defines Yeats's work into three periods and says 'much of his verse of all three periods is mystical and amatory. . . . It is important to emphasize that the preoccupation with love so apparent in his last poems was evident, just as his mysticism was evident, in his early work',[1] yet he does not make adequate use of even this summary generalization in looking at the poems of the decade 1929–39. Dr. Jeffares, is even less perceptive and makes only the most banal and perfunctory reference to the tormented, sex-obsessed work of the last years: 'There was no restriction on the expression of his feelings. If anything interested him then he wrote about it.' Academic thin-bloodedness could hardly falsify reality more seriously.

Richard Ellman, in his recent biography, *Yeats: The Man and The Masks*,[2] takes his cue from Dr. Bronowski's early essay and makes it central to his exposition of Yeats's 'ideas' in *A Vision*. He notes that:

'In the dedication to *A Vision* in 1925 he had admitted

[1] J. Hone, *W. B. Yeats*, 1865–1939, London, Macmillan, 1942.
[2] London, Macmillan & Co., Ltd., 1949,

that the book was not really finished, since he had said "little of sexual love" and nothing about the "Beatific Vision". The juxtaposition of the two subjects was not accidental for in sexual love he had an excellent symbol for the conflicting, interpenetrating gyres, while in the "conflagration of the whole being" of the sexual act he saw the antinomies resolved and the window open momentarily upon the Beatific Vision. . . . With Yeats the reader suspects that the poet may prefer the symbol of beatitude to beatitude itself. He had developed amazing power over his metaphors: the interpenetrating gyres are symbolic of sexual love, but it would be equally true to say that sexual love is symbolic of the gyres. . . .'

But what Ellman, like other critics sensitive to these features in Yeats' thought, has shirked is the *demonstration* of how in the range of gesture and action provided by sexual experience Yeats had defined for himself *a field of interest* upon which to improvise and from which to draw imaginative sustenance. Like the religious poets of the Christian tradition, of whom he is certainly not to be considered one, Yeats found in the language of sexual emotion a universally meaningful language for translating his apprehension of good. But once said, even this is inadequate. The critic's real responsibility is to show how all this *works* in the poems.

That this must be a more serious challenge than we sometimes allow is shown up by the most recent critical study of Yeats, Mr. Donald Stauffer's *The*

18

Golden Nightingale.[1] Only one of the last poems, 'The Gyres' is studied at any length and that for obvious reasons. For the rest, Mr. Stauffer contents himself with a series of generalizations about 'some principles of poetry in the lyrics', generalizations which reveal how far the critical task yet is from completion. Perhaps the most extraordinary assertion made by Mr. Stauffer is that the principle of Yeats' poetry is 'lyrical stasis'. Further, that

'The appreciation of his lyrics demands a criticism acknowledging that some forms of poetry are not essentially dramatic, that some poets cannot be considered as pastiches, that irony is not the sole secret of intensity or even comprehensiveness, and that analytical methods and the assumption of complexity (in the sense that a magpie's nest is complex) may betray the lyrical drive towards intense simplicity and compressed form.'

Since Mr. Stauffer's book will undoubtedly fall into the many eager hands awaiting help with Yeats's later work, it is necessary to question this passage proposition by proposition. Now, while some forms of poetry are not essentially dramatic, almost all of Yeats's poetry, to a singular degree, *is*. Second, *no* poems should ever be considered as pastiches; if they can be so considered, the critic can be sure they are not poems. Third, while it is true that irony is not the sole secret of intensity or even of comprehensiveness, I cannot remember that this touchstone has been over-applied to Yeats's poetry,

[1] New York, The Macmillan Company, 1949.

19

with the possible exception of Mr. Cleanth Brooks's study of one poem, 'Among Schoolchildren'. Most serious of all, is the shocking evasion of the critical task implied by Mr. Stauffer's curious statement that 'analytic methods and the assumption of complexity . . . may betray the lyrical drive toward intense simplicity and compressed form'. What other methods but analytic ones is the critic to use in the exploration of a work of art? And why should an 'assumption' of complexity be made about Yeats's poems, when they are, in fact, complex?

The oddest non-sequitur of the passage, which, one hopes, may stem from Mr. Stauffer's unhelpful syntax, is the statement that analytic methods in the critic, or his 'assumption of complexity' 'betray the lyrical drive'. Surely, it is only the poet himself who can betray the lyrical drive. Moreover, if what Mr. Stauffer is saying is that analysis of Yeats's lyrics (which sought an *effect* of simplicity), as if they were complex, will tend to abrogate the real nature of the poems, I think the experience of most persons with Yeats's poetry will refute that. Their simplicity is the simplicity of any self-contained work of art which is 'simple' in its unity and complex in its parts. *How* the complexities which all readers of Yeats have found in the poems, and especially in the last poems, get resolved by the *technical process* of art into an intense and single unit of experience—the poem—is something which Mr. Stauffer disappointingly does not show us in his study.

Considering the overwhelmingly biographical cast of recent Yeats studies, it seems incredible that no one has explicitly connected the temporary increase of sexual vitality resulting from the Steinach glandular operation, performed on Yeats in 1934, with the upsurge of interest in physical vitality to be seen in the last poems. And yet Yeats *was* dying. The real significance of the operation is not in its quite debatable effects on Yeats's personality, but the symptomatic gesture of his voluntary submission to an unorthodox operation whose aim was specifically to increase both longevity and sexual power. The extraordinary readiness with which Yeats accepted the validity of the then quite radical operation, and arranged for its performance only two weeks after he had first heard of it, is effectively suggested by Dr. Jeffares, although he is not concerned either to assess Yeats's motives or the operation's after-effects. Yet every scrap of the surrounding evidence, if the evidence of the poems themselves is not enough, in Yeats's letters, recorded remarks to friends, and direct statements shows that sexual energy was the source, subject and theme of the major poems of the last decade. It was only with difficulty that Mrs. Yeats persuaded him not to include the terrifyingly frank songs of 'The Three Bushes' in the small group of his own poems in the *Oxford Book of Modern Verse* he was compiling in 1935.

But to see in this poetry only a simple 'affirmation' of sex, or worse, of sensuality is narrow, when it is not vulgar. In sexual experience, as I have suggested, Yeats found the energy, the imagery and the basic antinomies of mortality organized into an intricate and tragic nexus. The man who at seventy-one could write from his sick-bed to his younger friend, Lady Gerald Wellesley: 'The first and last sense, and the second mystery—the mystery that touches the genitals, a blurred touch through a curtain . . .', was not musing aimlessly. For the very next day, (9th November 1936) the observation has translated itself into a poem. Yeats writes to Dorothy Wellesley: 'After I had written to you I tried to find better words to explain what I meant by the touch from behind the curtain. This morning, this came.' Then is quoted the first version of the Lover's song in the moving sequence which later became 'The Three Bushes'. A few days later Yeats was writing the strange, sensual music of the Chambermaid's two songs. The sequence, about which there has been an extraordinarily critical silence considering both its length and its merit, shows Yeats following the sexual theme through its various manifestations. Out of the seemingly random observation of 9th November had grown a sequence of seven powerful poems, at least three of them among the boldest 'love' lyrics ever written.

But it is essential to see Yeats's sexuality only as the source and not as the end of the last poems. The 'animal wisdom' which he attributes to Dorothy Wellesley's poem, 'Matrix', and which makes him 'jealous' of it, he sees as a philosophical attribute. It was, he wrote, 'the most moving philosophic poem of our time . . . precisely because its wisdom bulked animal below the waist. . . .' Out of the great pain of his early sexual frustration (the moving confessions concerning his seven years' celibacy in the unpublished autobiography quoted by Dr. Jeffares are unforgettable: 'I was tortured with sexual desire and disappointed love. Often as I walked in the woods at Coole it would have been a relief to have screamed aloud.') Yeats arrived at a compensatory and perhaps desperate over-emphasis on the sexual good in his old age. But he made it, as he made all his themes, into something more than the revelation of a personal agony.

Still, the personal roots were deep. He could write to Dorothy Wellesley just before completing 'The Three Bushes': 'Forgive all this my dear but I have told you that my poetry all comes from rage or lust.' And of the poem he wrote and named for her, he explains: 'I did not plan it deliberately. That conflict (of the poem) is deep in my subconscious, perhaps in everybody's. I dream of clear water, perhaps two or three times (the moon of the poem), then come erotic dreams. Then for weeks perhaps I write poetry with sex for a theme. . . .' Only two years before his death, Yeats, in a letter which shows the fevered intensity of his feeling, had been subdued into a chaster one, touchingly writes that he had come out of the 'Darkness' [he had been ill] with the recognition that he has lost her. 'For part of my solitude was that I felt I would never know that supreme experience of life—that I think possible to the young—to share profound thought and then to touch.' When Dorothy Wellesley comes to edit these letters her own laconic notes, made during Yeats's visits to her home during the time of the friendship, say much: 'Sex, Philosophy and the Occult continue to preoccupy him. He strangely intermingles all

23

three.'[1] It is useful to notice the order of her list. The significance of 'intermingles' is self-evident.

The preoccupation is everywhere. When some broadcasts on modern poetry were proposed for the BBC in 1936 Yeats wrote, in accepting: 'My preliminary statement would explain that the theme was love.' And, later, when he was about to broadcast with the painter Dulac, he presented his thesis with a disarming naïveté: 'That it is not the duty of the artist to paint beautiful women is nonsense. That the exclusion of sex appeal from poetry, painting and sculpture is nonsense (are the films alone to impose their ideas upon the sexual instinct?) that, on the contrary, all arts are an expression of desire—exciting desirable life, exalting desirable death.'

But when one uses words like 'preoccupation' the impulse to examine Yeats's work in the light of these facts may, to the careless, seem clinical rather than critical. Nothing, in fact, could be further from my intention. The sexual theme is of significance as the final symbolic statement of that creative conflict which Yeats had early posited as the dynamic of the universe. In the *Autobiographies* he had written: 'All creation is from conflict, whether, with our own minds or with that of others, and the historian who dreams of bloodless victory, wrongs the wounded veteran.' By the time of *A Vision* Yeats had extended his early notion of strife as the principle of the artistic process (the idea of the Mask was one term of this conflict, standing for the *willed* image of the self) to a more universal prin-

[1] *W. B. Yeats: Letters on Poetry to Dorothy Wellesly*, London, Oxford University Press, 1940.

24

ciple. In the cosmological system of *A Vision* Phase 1 and Phase 28 are described as being without human incarnations because human life is impossible without strife between the 'tinctures'.[1] And Unity of Being, the most desired state in the hierarchy of personality, is significantly centred in the sexual life:

'Hitherto we have been part of something else, but now discover everything in our own nature. Sexual love becomes the most important event in life, for the opposite sex is nature chosen and fated. . . . Every emotion begins to be related to every other as musical notes are related.'

The marriage-bed alone is seen as the 'symbol of the solved antinomy' of the irreconcilable conflict at the heart of living. It 'were more than symbol could a man there lose and keep his identity, but he falls asleep. That sleep is the same as death'. And death cannot solve this Kantian antinomy whose thesis is freedom, and antithesis, necessity. For in Yeats's view, death and life are themselves the expression of the opposition. The young man who had vexed his father by defining truth as 'the dramatically appropriate' became the poet who saw in sex the dramatically appropriate range of speech, gesture and feeling to exploit the irreconcilable strife which he saw as the fulcrum of the human condition. It is this deep motive which gives the imagery of the

[1] Yeats appears to owe his use of this term to its standard meaning in alchemical literature as an 'immaterial quintessential native principle' capable of causing material and spiritual changes. The alchemists, however, believed the tinctures had to be infused to bring about such changes.

last poems such a tremendous hold on our hearts and our imaginations. For 'we begin to live when we conceive life as tragedy'.

Even the abstract and conventional symbols of gyres, cones, phases, of *A Vision*[1] referred, in the end, to the human situation. After developing an elaborate terminology, elucidated by ingenious and equally arbitrary diagrams, Yeats tells us at the end of his work: 'All these symbols can be thought of as the symbols of the relations of men and women and the birth of children . . . all the symbolism of this book applies to begetting and birth, for all things are a single form which has divided and multiplied in time and place.' It is this interest which is at the centre of Yeats's last poems. But the limits of this symbolic order are hinted at in more than one place. And not the least of these is in Yeats' reported remark to John Sparrow: 'The tragedy of sexual intercourse is in the perpetual virginity of the soul.'

When we come to the last poems, then, we must not forget that Yeats was writing out of the deepest necessities of his personality. The early 'Mask' was no longer an actively operative ideal. It is Yeats who is looking through the eyes of all the Lunatic Toms and Crazy Janes and Wild Old Wicked Men. Contrary to the notion Eliot has made so persuasive in our time, the man who suffered and the man who wrote were, in the most creative sense of suffering, *one*. But what was precipitated by this purgative fire—the poems—is the real pretext for my comments.

[1] I quote always from the 1937 edition of *A Vision*, longer by at least 100 pages than the privately printed version of 1925.

GROUP ONE

1. THE WILD OLD WICKED MAN

2. AN ACRE OF GRASS

THE WILD OLD WICKED MAN

'Because I am mad about women
I am mad about the hills,'
Said that wild old wicked man
Who travels where God wills.
'Not to die on the straw at home,
Those hands to close these eyes,
That is all I ask, my dear,
From the old man in the skies.
            Daybreak and a candle-end.

'Kind are all your words, my dear,
Do not the rest withhold.
Who can know the year, my dear,
When an old man's blood grows cold?
I have what no young man can have
Because he loves too much.
Words I have that can pierce the heart,
But what can he do but touch?'
            Daybreak and a candle-end.

Then said she to that wild old man,
His stout stick under his hand,
'Love to give or to withhold
Is not at my command.
I gave it all to an older man:

That old man in the skies.
Hands that are busy with His beads
Can never close those eyes.'
Daybreak and a candle-end.

Go your ways, O go your ways,
I choose another mark,
Girls down on the seashore
Who understand the dark;
Bawdy talk for the fishermen;
A dance for the fisher-lads;
When dark hangs upon the water
They turn down their beds.
Daybreak and a candle-end.

'A young man in the dark am I,
But a wild old man in the light,
That can make a cat laugh, or
Can touch by mother wit
Things hid in their marrow-bones
From time long passed away,
Hid from all those warty lads
That by their bodies lay.
Daybreak and a candle-end.

'All men live in suffering,
I know as few can know,
Whether they take the upper road
Or stay content on the low,
Rower bent in his row-boat
Or weaver bent at his loom,

Horseman erect upon horseback
Or child hid in the womb.
        Daybreak and a candle-end.

'That some stream of lightning
From the old man in the skies
Can burn out that suffering
No right-taught man denies.
But a coarse old man am I,
I choose the second-best,
I forget it all awhile
Upon a woman's breast.'
        Daybreak and a candle-end.

I

THE WILD OLD WICKED MAN

I have chosen this poem to begin with because it expresses what is really behind the varied conventions of
the poems written between 1934 and 1939. Whether
these poems are cast in ballad form, whether the fictive
point of view is a mad woman's, a lover's, or an old
man's, whether the tone is exultant or ironic, the
prevalent energy in them is always the same. I mean
the energy of suffering. Dr. Jeffares blandly writes of
the almost terrifying poem we are now to study, that
it 'had a certain autobiographical flavour, being written
to a friend of his'.[1]

'The Wild Old Wicked Man' expresses directly what
the Crazy Jane poems, begun almost a decade before,
had got at obliquely: 'All men live in suffering.' But
we must remark that the force of 'live' in this poem,
coming before the caesura, as it does, and benefiting
further by the rising accent of the metre, is that of the
most important word in the line. Its position in the
line reveals Yeats's intention to stress the fact that
the condition of living is to suffer. But this is not all.
The placing of the word suggests a further ambiguity.
It is that man is only truly [a]*live* in suffering, that is to
say, in conflict, challenge and a continual testing of the
resources of the self rather than in a passive endurance

---

[1] Lady Elizabeth Pelham.

of circumstance. It was because of this belief that Yeats could not be persuaded to include Wilfred Owen, perhaps the best of the war poets, in his *Oxford Book of Modern Verse*, holding that passive suffering was not a subject for poetry. In this connection, his letter to Dorothy Wellesley describing the nature of this necessary inner struggle is illuminating:

'We all have something within ourselves to batter down and get our power from this fighting. I have never produced a play in verse without showing the actors that the passion of the verse comes from the fact that the speakers are holding down violence or madness—down "Hysterico passio". All depends on the completeness of the holding down, on the stirring of the beast beneath.'

In 'The Wild Old Wicked Man', the dialogue pattern of the traditional ballad, as well as its regular refrain, stabilizes the turbulent experience it contains. Thus formalized into a familiar shape, it does not repel, or put off the reader as do the freer-in-form 'songs' of 'The Three Bushes'. In advising Dorothy Wellesley about her own poetry, Yeats wrote: 'Then look up any old book of ballads and you will find that they have all perfectly regular rhyme schemes. . . . In narrative verse we want to concentrate the attention on the fact of the story, not on the form. The form must be present as something we all accept—"the fundamental sing-song". I do not know of a single example of good narrative where the rhyme scheme is varied.'

When we come to look at the imagery of 'The Wild

Old Wicked Man' we find that it is almost exclusively sexual. This is not accidental. Whether consciously or unconsciously arrived at, the inevitability of the selection is implicit, as in all powerful imagery. When we do not sense this inevitability, we are uncomfortable, or, worse, unpersuaded of the reality of the experience it is meant to dramatize. The mocking refrain of this poem, itself a summary of the theme, is '*Daybreak and a candle-end*'. The incomplete anapaestic last foot trails off into a frustration suggested by the cognate meanings of the symbol of the candle-end: maleness deposed, the end of vitality, the extinction of a principle, in short, which illuminates experience. This, as well as the whole complex of conventional associations which cling to the concrete facts of a burnt candle and a cold dawn all combine into a bleak and ironic acceptance of personal extinction—death—as terminus.

Here all the customary trimmings of Yeats's somewhat puny will-to-believe in personal immortality are abandoned. For a 'right-taught' man (again we must weigh the metric emphasis on 'right') can have his suffering alleviated by the old man in the skies, but the singer is not one of these:

> 'But a coarse old man am I,
> I choose the second-best
> I forget it all while
> Upon a woman's breast.'
> *Daybreak and a candle-end.*

These closing lines, so moving in their humility and their humanness, achieve a heightened poignance by the comfortless refrain. In fact, the italics of the refrain are a measure of its value as antithesis. The oblivion to be found on a woman's breast is the death-sleep of the marriage-bed Yeats had written of in *A Vision*.

But there are additional technical supports which contribute to the moving action of this strange lyric. First, we must notice how masterly is Yeats's syntax in setting up the persuasive agency which a poem is—if we are to share in the poet's experience:

> *Because* I am mad about women
> I am mad about the hills[1]

To start the poem like this pleads for our acceptance of the reasonableness of the speaker's judgment. At the same time, by putting the seemingly subordinate clause first, the real theme is emphasized: it is the speaker's madness for women and not his madness for the hills. It is interesting to note that in spite of the fact that in his middle work Yeats left off the traditional inversions of romantic diction (he had come to hate 'The Lake Isle of Innisfree' because of this reliance) and in spite of the advice he was giving Dorothy Wellesley against using inversions, he himself uses them whenever he chooses. But, as we shall see in the analysis of 'An Acre of Grass', the inversion is always for emphasis. In 'The Wild Old Wicked Man' inversion is a sustained device which helps create the archaic texture of an authentic ballad. More focally, the inversions *help the argument*:

> 'Words I have that can pierce the heart'

[1] Italics mine.

or

'Love to give or withhold'.

In the first instance, by inverting the normal word order it is almost as if 'Words' were italicized, so much stress do we give it in reading. The speaker is Yeats, the poet. He is proud of his words. They are the gift he offers to the woman. Similarly, the mono-syllabic accented 'love' of the woman's reply, because of its displacement from the ordinary word-sequence, emphasizes its primacy to her scheme. Love is what she has to deal out.

Earlier in the poem, the inversion in 'Kind are all your words, my dear' lends 'kind' an extraordinary irony. If we try to substitute 'All your words are kind, my dear' the distinction in tone is shown up. For the wild old wicked man doesn't want kindness; he wants 'the rest'. And his argument is no conventional 'Carpe diem' to the withholding lady but the tragic recognition of his own imminent non-being:

Who can know the year, my dear,
When an old man's blood grows cold?

To return to the symbols of the poem: The hills represent the wildness and the loneliness of the terrain which is *home* to the old man. But hills are also a common male symbol and, as such, they dramatize the old man's most consuming interest, as well as his biographical identity with the poet himself, who dwells among the high, hilly places of the violent intellect. The sexual

37

quality of the symbolism is even bolder in the next stanza:

> Then said she to the wild old man
> His stout stick under his hand

The lady may be religious; her devotions are not to this old man, with 'His stout stick under his hand'. While the phallic nature of this image is obvious, it also works at the literal level of the fiction that the poet is an old man striding among the hills where he would of course need a stick to help him. But the sense of stick (phallus) as man's support is primary; it is central to Yeats's values at this time.

There has been much discussion of Yeats's utilization of folk materials in the early and early-middle poems. But the way in which these materials were later sublimated to the total poetic movement, rather than providing the fable of the poem itself, has not yet been adequately investigated. In this poem the folk-content is significant. It helps the symbolism, while at the same time figuring in maintaining the fiction of the poem. When the wild old man bids the too other-worldly lady to 'Go your ways, O go your ways' and chooses instead 'Girls down on the seashore who understand the dark', he recommends his powers of love-making and of prophecy. He can release in these girls

> 'Things hid in their marrowbones
> From time long passed away
> Hid from all those warty lads
> That by their body lay.

The adjective 'warty', so grossly colloquial, provides exactly the right realistic leavening to this otherwise slightly vague boast. Its homeliness heightens by contrast the old man's claim to qualities so different. But it enriches both senses of 'warty' to know that in Irish folk-belief warts are connected with sexual potency, as Yeats explains in a letter to Dorothy Wellesley. The passage further illuminates Yeats's tendency to see the creative function in sexual terms, and while it does not refer to 'The Wild Old Wicked Man', it incidentally enriches our reading of it:

'I wrote to Laura Riding to-day . . . that her school was too thoughtful, reasonable and truthful, that poets were good liars who never forget that the Muses were women who liked the embrace of gay warty lads. I wonder if she knows that warts are considered by the Irish peasantry a sign of sexual power.'

The wild old man's wish in stanza one 'Not to die on the straw at home' is also understandable without reference to folk-lore. But its meaning is heightened if we know that 'strawdeath' is commonly considered in Gaelic (Irish and Scottish) belief to be an ignominious death, while the honourable death is one of violence. In Scotland, the term 'straedeath' is still common among the miners. But the real import of both 'warty' and 'Die on the straw' is that both work with almost the full impact of their more obscure referents simply because of their place and function in the context. When this happens, when the word is for reasons of its dramatic inter-action with contiguous words the

39

best word, there can never be a question of 'obscurity', even if the ultimate referent in experience private to the poet not is distinguished. The importance of this principle will be illustrated in the more 'obscure' poems, the 'rich, dark' poems, which are less amenable to biographic or linguistic research. It is, among other things, their recalcitrance to extra-poetic filling-in which has put off the fuller study of these poems.

It is a significant feature of many of the last poems, particularly those which are cast into ballad form, that the refrain is turned into a question, thus leaving the problem or theme of the poem unresolved. 'What Then?' or 'The Curse of Cromwell' are good illustrations of this practice. But 'The Wild Old Wicked Man' answers all the questions concerning personal immortality raised by the poem. There is solace possible for the 'right-taught' who recognize the old man in the skies who 'Can burn out suffering'. But for others there is an alternative stated flatly and with a crude forthrightness to 'forget it all awhile/Upon a woman's breast'.

This, then, is one poem where Yeats is not poised in a great irresolution over the paradox of sensuality and the spirit, a problem that held him to the end. Here, for once, he is settled in a *choice*, even if it is an ironic 'second-best', grateful, as he put it in a letter to Dorothy Wellesley, for 'body's stupidity'. But even so, the solution is not complacent. It is only for an imperfect 'while' that man can forget that 'All men live in suffering'. The great healing agency of sex is only a temporary, or, should we say, temporal, help. The mocking limitation of this knowledge, after the bravely chosen 'second-best' comes in the final harsh '*Daybreak and a candle-end*'. It was now, at life's end, that Dawn or, as he put it elsewhere, 'the terrible novelty of light' challenged Yeats with a heightened intensity.

AN ACRE OF GRASS

Picture and book remain,
An acre of green grass
For air and exercise
Now strength of body goes;
Midnight, an old house
Where nothing stirs but a mouse.

My temptation is quiet.
Here at life's end
Neither loose imagination,
Nor the mill of the mind
Consuming its rag and bone,
Can make the truth known.

Grant me an old man's frenzy,
Myself must I remake
Till I am Timon and Lear
Or that William Blake
Who beat upon the wall
Till Truth obeyed his call.

A mind Michael Angelo knew
That can pierce the clouds,
Or inspired by frenzy
Shake the dead in their shrouds;
Forgotten else by mankind,
An old man's eagle mind.

AN ACRE OF GRASS

This poem presents the other side of the coin to the theme of 'The Wild Old Wicked Man', and can be thought of as both supplementary and complementary to it. The mood of the opening lines is not unlike that of the ending of 'The Wild Old Wicked Man'. The powerful incantatory vehicle of the poem is established at once in the grave beginning, with its acceptance of the inevitable physical degradation of age:

> Now strength of body goes;
> Midnight, an old house
> Where nothing stirs but a mouse.

But the superb first line of the next stanza introduces a new note: 'My temptation is quiet'. Here Yeats relinquishes that oppressive concern with the impossible union of the marriage-bed which so bedevilled him in his last days. The line *is* quiet. The alternative temptation, *not* to accept one's decline in the face of objective evidence, is subdued. Instead, the poet asks for the capacity to remake himself in the image of those old men who possess 'frenzy' appropriate to old men. 'Frenzy', which Louis MacNeice rightly sees as the key-word of the poem,[1] is an elastic word. It covers a

[1] In *The Poetry of W. B. Yeats*, London, Oxford University Press, 1941.

process, or, rather, a progress in Yeats's search for the philosopher's stone. His longing to achieve mystical vision, dating from the early days of his cabalistic interests, through the later psychic 'research' and up to the 'system' attempted in *A Vision* is here dramatized as the will-to-frenzy.

Dr. Jeffares writes of this poem:

'Truth, as represented by the frenzy of an old man, means a position with the great frenzied minds of the past, "forgotten else by mankind". This thought was suggested by Nietzsche to whom Yeats had returned at the end of the nineteen-thirties; it is an echo of a passage in "The Dawn of Day" which states that elderly people, through a love of enjoyment, wish to enjoy the results of their thinking, rather than testing them.'

To so emasculate the religious fervour of this poem in favour of a simple 'influence' is to rob it of its own symbolic richness. If we must import matter from outside the poem, there is a source closer at hand than Nietzsche. For this is one of the instances where *A Vision* can help us. Under Phase 16, The Positive Man (which, characteristically, includes 'some beautiful women'), Yeats describes the violence of types like Blake and Rabelais in whom there is some element of frenzy and whose

'hate is always close to madness. These men discover symbolism to express the overflowing and bursting of the mind . . . a delight in certain glowing or shining images of concentrated force: in the smith's forge; in

46

the heart; in the human form in its most vigorous development; in the solar disc; in some symbolical representation of the sexual organs; for the being must brag of its triumph over its incoherence.'

It is clear from this passage that it is exactly for opposite reasons than the ones Dr. Jeffares supposes that Yeats has chosen to align himself with these old men. They are the old men who are not content to rest on their laurels but with an energy that resembles madness continue to push through the conventional boundaries of apprehension. Timon, Lear, and William Blake are men whose minds 'can pierce the clouds'. 'Pierce' is the antithesis of the diffuse, ineffectual thought of the 'loose imagination' of old men who do not possess frenzy. 'Loose' is an especially telling word because it is a concrete feature to put against a faculty so abstract as 'imagination'. It evokes the shambling, drooling inadequacy of old age's physical pattern and translates it to the man's inner functioning. And just as 'loose imagination' cannot 'make the truth known' neither can the 'mill of the mind'. Here Yeats takes over Blake's symbol of the Mill which stands for the mechanical, routine iteration of the industrial machine, but he extends it to 'mill of the mind', that mode of habitual and uncreative thinking which he had always despised.

The technical brilliance of this short lyric produces the purity and incandescence of a Shakespearean song. It transcends these qualities in Yeats's earlier 'little Mechanical Songs' for it projects a clarity of statement those more mantic poems in the Blake style do not, possibly because they were not meant to. A technical feature I should like to examine are the inversions. I have already pointed out how freely Yeats reversed his own advice on this practice. But it is worth noting that as early as between 1887 and 1891 Yeats already was questioning the correctness of the conventional poetic syntax of his own work. In 'The Trembling of the Veil' he recalls:

'I had begun to loosen rhythm as an escape from rhetoric and from that emotion of the crowd that rhetoric brings, but I only understood vaguely that I must for my special purpose use nothing but the common syntax. . . . A couple of years later I would not have written [in "The Lake Isle of Innisfree"] . . . the inversion in the last stanza.'

It is worth glancing at that poem to see what Yeats objected to in it. The inversion he mentions, 'While I stand on the road or on the pavements grey', by displacing the adjective makes possible a chiming end-rhyme with 'day', as well as an internal rhyme with 'roadway'. But it was not until 1914, possibly under the bracing self-criticism which his friendship with Ezra Pound had brought about, that Yeats decided that he must, once and for all, abandon the inversions of his early romantic diction. There, inversion merely permits a disturbance of normal word order for the sake of end-rhyme. Forty years later, inversion becomes a device for 'intensity', never for convenience or 'poeticality'. Let us see how it works.

48

In 'An Acre of Grass' the normal speech order, an order Yeats now theoretically placed highest, would be 'I must remake myself'. The first displacement would give us 'Myself I must remake'. Here the importance of the 'self', as the object of remaking, is got because it has the strong accent of the iambic foot and an arresting position at the beginning of the line. To stress 'self' is to make it felt as a manipulable part of personality, open to alteration from other forces in the psyche. This relation expresses brilliantly Yeats's early concept of the Will and the Mask. But if the normal word-order were not even further altered, two additional effects would be sacrificed: first, the alliterative re-enforcement of 'Myself' by 'must'; second, the wilful asseveration which is got by placing 'must' where it gets the initial beat in the spondaic foot 'must I'. It is the *mustness* which tells, by its position, the urgency of the intention.

Let me direct this syntactic break-down to another feature of Yeats's diction: his use of connectives. The colloquial connective 'till' in the following line is a remarkable strategy. A study of his connectives alone, I suspect, would underline one of the secrets of the exceptional persuasiveness of his poetry (to say nothing of its 'flow'), a persuasiveness that grows from the cunning of a man to whom speech-making was a respectable intellectual discipline, and oratory a serious art. Here 'till' implies that the process of remaking is a gradual one, that it is not achieved by a single burst of energy, and that there is a *scale* of growth, the very apex of which is 'piercing' the clouds (that is, vision).

Thus, 'till' works a subtle change upon our credulity. It makes us accept the *reality* of the change. We can believe, just because it does represent it as the end-point of a serial development, that such a transcendence of personality is really possible and not merely a wished-for condition. The present tense 'am', monosyllabic and formal, hastens our conviction that this transfiguration has indeed come about.

The next syntactic feature that deserves notice is the use of the demonstrative adjective in line four of the same stanza: 'Or that William Blake'. In the light of the surrounding context 'that' is not merely the usual pointer. Here it isolates the aspect of Blake which Yeats is stressing—the almost superhuman Blake who, for the moment, takes on the lineaments of divinity which we see in the terrible Heavenly figures of his drawings, and becomes himself Godlike. But without the demonstrative 'that' the intense reality of this picture would be diminished. As Mr. G. Rostrevor Hamilton suggests in his interesting essay, 'The Tell-Tale Article',[1] the definite article in poetry 'is very commonly used for the direct presentation of a picture or idea which wins our recognition the moment it is put before us'. But, I should like to add, the demonstrative *adjective* is even more specific in the limitations it imposes on the uniqueness, the particularity of the thing pointed to. Substitute 'the' for 'that' in the above line and the weakening of both immediacy and meaning is instantaneous.

Mr. Hamilton's further contention that an over-

[1] *The Tell-Tale Article*, London, William Heinemann Ltd., 1949.

abundance of the definite article in much poetry of the nineteen–thirties weakens its structural support—that is, the one given by verbs and relative clauses—is equally suggestive. If we proceed along similar lines of observation, we find that in 'An Acre of Grass' out of the total of 116 words only five are the definite article, making a percentage of less than 5 per cent. Among the moderns, Mr. Hamilton finds that the definite article often accounts for as much as 10 per cent or more of the poem's total word-count. Interestingly, of the various English poets whom Mr. Hamilton studies, only Donne has less than 2 per cent of the definite article. The figure for all of Yeats's poems would no doubt vary sharply from that of *An Acre of Grass*', but I think it would not be difficult to establish by count that there is a break in practice from about 1914 (*Responsibilities*) and on, with an increasing suppression of the definite article so that in the *Last Poems* we have a linguistic texture almost as tightly knit as Donne's, although not comparable in tone.

Now, what we should wish to remember is the *effect* of this habit in the poetry, rather than the miracle of the economy for its own sake. When Mr. Hamilton writes of Donne that the infrequency of the definite article 'has a significant relation to his style and method . . . the force of his plain virile speech' while 'adjectives are relatively few, and are employed not for decorative effect but for sharp essential strokes of meaning' we are at once struck by the likeness this bears to Yeats's comment to Dorothy Wellesley: 'You get much of your effect from a spare use of the adjective. . . . It gives your work objectivity.' And in *Dramatis Personae*, he wrote at about the same time (1935) that 'in dramatizing some possible singer or speaker we must remember that he is moved by one thing at a time (and) certain words must be dull and numb. Here and there in early poems I have introduced[1] such numbness and dullness . . . that all might seem remembered with indifference except one vivid image.'

Another feature of the great rhetorical power of 'An Acre of Grass', a poem which is not untypical of the structural pattern of Yeats's later diction, is the fluent line of the argument. The poem breaks naturally into halves. The first half is a description of the speaker's situation at life's end. The second is a prayer for 'an old man's frenzy'. The supplication of the opening 'Grant me an old man's frenzy' is parenthetically amplified by the next five lines of the stanza. The first line of the last stanza connects with 'Grant me an old man's frenzy' and is, in fact, in apposition with it. This effects a stanzaic rather than a linear *enjambement*. To achieve such fluency, a fluency of argument which Mr. Hamilton, following Matthew Arnold, sees as one of the distinctive features of the English lyric tradition, Yeats, like Donne, utilizes a large number of relative clauses: 'Who beat upon the wall', 'That can pierce the clouds', etc.

And, serving the same end, there is also the device of disjunction, which allows Yeats to pile up his par-

---

[1] This *post-facto* habit of Yeats has annoyed some of his scholar-critics who would rather have the less perfect poem but have it perfectly datable.

ticulars in a fluent series without an over-reliance on 'and'. Note, for example, the serial flow made possible by '*Neither* loose imagination,/*Nor* the mill of the mind', and '*Or* that William Blake', '*Or* inspire by frenzy'.[1] An additional syntactic feature Yeats shares with Donne, and certainly not the least in the sense it conveys of the immediacy of the experience (it also eliminates the need for the definite article), is the frequent use of the possessive: 'life's end', 'old man's frenzy', 'old man's eagle mind'.

But perhaps the most crucial syntactic principle to observe is that poetry as passionate and concentrated as this will naturally contrive its thrust with the aid of powerful verbs. This poem is no exception. The verbs of the first half are intransitive and thus adapted to the relaxed tone of its statement: 'remain', 'goes', 'stirs'. The verbs of the second half, the plea for vision, are largely imperative in mood, predominantly mono-syllabic, and sharply kinetic: 'Grant', 'must', 'remake', 'beat', 'obeyed', 'Pierce', and 'shake', to mention only the most outstanding.

This remarkable battery of verbs is another technical sign of the essentially didactic quality of Yeats's lyric-ism. When we remember his early conviction that Truth is 'dramatically appropriate utterance' and his later belief that there must be the dramatic fiction of a speaker or singer to whom this utterance is appropriate, we see that within the self-conscious limits offered by this convention Yeats found it possible to disguise his didactic intention in a lyric or dramatic or lyric-drama-

[1] Italics mine.

tic texture. Possibly the best way to put this complex relationship is to say that the 'intensity' of Yeats's lyricism (of which the verbs are only one aspect) is the function of its didactic urge. The fusion of these two motives, it seems to me, is always present in the greatest poetry, and to recognize it is to do away with standard categories of poetry like 'lyric', 'didactic', or 'dramatic'.

GROUP TWO

1. THE STATUES

2. A BRONZE HEAD

THE STATUES

Pythagoras planned it. Why did the people stare?
His numbers, though they moved or seemed to move
In marble or in bronze, lacked character.
But boys and girls pale from the imagined love
Of solitary beds, knew what they were,
That passion could bring character enough,
And pressed at midnight in some public place
Live lips upon a plummet-measured face.

No! Greater than Pythagoras, for the men
That with a mallet or a chisel modelled these
Calculations that look but casual flesh, put down
All Asiatic vague immensities,
And not the banks of oars that swam upon
The many-headed foam at Salamis.
Europe put off that foam when Phidias
Gave women dreams and dreams their looking-glass.

One image crossed the many-headed, sat
Under the tropic shade, grew round and slow,
No Hamlet thin from eating flies, a fat
Dreamer of the Middle Ages. Empty eyeballs knew
That knowledge increases unreality, that
Mirror on mirror mirrored is all the show.
When gong and conch declare the hour to bless
Grimalkin crawls to Buddha's emptiness.

When Pearse summoned Cuchulain to his side,
What stalked through the Post Office? What intellect,
What calculation, number, measurement, replied?
We Irish, born into that ancient sect
But thrown upon this filthy modern tide
And by its formless spawning fury wrecked,
Climb to our proper dark, that we may trace
The lineaments of a plummet-measured face.

THE STATUES

'The Statues' is a superb poem which falls into the 'rich, dark' class. It is a poem which, quite understandably, has not been discussed for it presents a uniform front of obscurity which must prove irritating even to admirers of Yeats. But, happily, it is one poem, increasingly few among the *Last Poems*, which the relative clarity of Yeats's prose in *A Vision* and elsewhere helps to illumine. Of course, the real critical test of the obscurity would be to see just how far the poem 'worked' without this resource. What reading could be got alone without prose props? Still, to obstruct the use of electric light merely because one wants to prove that one *can* read by candle-light is a wasteful pastime. Once the body of an artist's thought and work is known to the critic, it is impossible to assume a fictive 'innocence', no matter how desirable innocence may be for independent and fresh responses.

'The Statues' might almost serve as a casebook example of the organic quality of creative experience. In this poem, written in 1938, less than a year before his death, Yeats's imagination dredges up images and observations from as far as thirty and forty years back. Let us begin with two of the most puzzling passages:

> One image crossed the many-headed, sat
> Under the tropic shade, grew round and slow,

No Hamlet thin from eating flies, a fat
Dreamer of the Middle Ages . . .

In the essay 'Four Years', dealing with his life between
1887–91, Yeats describes a reproduction of William
Morris' portrait by Watts which hung over his mantle
at the time he was writing these retrospective essays in
the early twenties:

'Its grave open eyes, like the eyes of some dreaming
beast, remind me of the open eyes of Titian's 'Ariosto',[1]
while the broad vigorous body suggests a mind that
has no need of the intellect to remain sane, although
it gives itself to every phantasy: It is the fool of fairy
. . . wide and wild as a hill, the resolute European
image that yet half remembers Buddha's motionless
speculation, and has no trait in common with the
wavering, lean image of Speculation, that cannot but
because of certain famous Hamlets of our stage fill the
mind's eye.'

The 'fat dreamer of the Middle Ages' would seem to
be a fusion in Yeats's mind of Titian's 'Ariosto', William Morris, and Buddha into a single image which
stood for the antithesis of the self-torn, intellectual
Western psyche represented by a Hamlet eating flies—
that is, feeding on the pestilential parasites of intellect.
The fact that Buddha's lifetime was some ten centuries
remote from the Middle Ages did not trouble Yeats's
flexible and somewhat arbitrary historical sense.

[1] A painting which Yeats loved and which had dominated his
youth.

But there was an even older layer of association that went into this conception of an organic, joyous wholeness which is the concept celebrated in this poem. During the years 1887–91 Yeats, while studying at the British Museum, often admired the statues there of Mausolus and Artemesia. These figures

'private, half-animal, half-divine figures, all unlike the Grecian athletes and Egyptian kings in their near neighbourhood . . . became to me . . . images of an unpremeditated joyous energy, that neither I nor any other man racked by doubt and inquiry can achieve . . . and I wanted to create once more an art where the artist's handiwork would hide as under those half-anonymous chisels. . . .'

And this notion of an anonymous creativity, deriving from the most organic sources of energy, was re-enforced in Yeats' mind by the private value he put upon Maud Gonne's special type of bodily beauty:

'. . . her face, like the face of some Greek statue, showed little thought, as though a Scopas had measured and long calculated, consorted with Egyptian sages and mathematicians out of Babylon, that he might face even Artemesia's sepulchral image with a living norm.

'But in that ancient civilization abstract thought scarce existed, while she rose but partially and but for a moment out of raging abstraction; and for that reason, as I have known another woman do, she hated her own beauty, not its effect upon others, but its image in the mirror. Beauty is from the antithetical self and a woman can scarce but hate it, for not only does it

61

demand a painful daily service, but it calls for the denial of self.'

This passage must be put against the whole of 'The Statues' which, complex though it is, nevertheless finds its centre in the antithesis Yeats makes between thoughtlessness and abstraction. The adjective 'raging' in the passage above dramatizes the destructive power Yeats attributed to the latter kind of thinking. Maud Gonne, William Morris, and Cuchulain, the latter no less real because in the heroic past, are the particulars he chooses as the materials of his own abstraction about abstractions.

Yeats's own description of this poem makes the theme seem vague enough. In a letter to Dorothy Wellesley on 10th June 1938, Yeats wrote: 'I have finished my long meditative poem about Greek statues.' The poem was sent to her in a letter of 22nd June, but there is no further comment on it. But merely to take the poem as 'about' Greek statues is to deny its rich particularity. For in it are united Yeats's ideas about the anonymity of Greek sculpture, the qualities of active and passive intellect, women as works of art, the endurance of the spirit after death (Cuchulain), and the spirit's accessibility as a source of energy to the contemporaneous world if it accepts its 'proper' historical role—here, the Irish rejecting the filthy modern tide.

The factual genesis of the poem—if this is not too crude a way to put it—goes back some fifty years to the seemingly trivial observation Yeats had made of the 'staring empty eyeballs' of Greek statues. This small detail eventually expands into a contrast between ancient and modern culture. But to call this process of uniting the particular and the general in experience 'myth' does not heighten one's pleasure nor add to one's understanding of the poem. In this connection, Peter Ure, perhaps the ablest critic of Yeats' poetry, writes: 'In the myth passion and abstraction join hands, the individual and the type cohere in a unity of balance. . . . In "The Statues" the creation of myth is indeed the pressing of live lips upon a plummet-measured face.'[1] Still, if one puts these two assertions against one another, we get the following equation: In 'The Statues' passion (Yeats's subjective regard of Maud Gonne as the incarnation of the Greek classical ideal in sculpture), joins hands with Yeats's abstraction concerning the *anonymous* perfection of classical art, and so results in a myth which is 'The Statues'. I cannot see that this hypothesis serves any useful purpose. Almost any poem in which the particular and general unite, and this happens in many poems, would then be 'myth'. To be so generous in assigning myth robs this lately over-fashionable concept of any validity it may yet confer.

Rather than to call 'The Statues' a myth and to let the critical challenge go at that, I should like to consider certain aspects of its craftsmanship more amenable to objective inspection. First, the *tone* of the poem requires comment. It is prophetic, and prophetic in

[1] See *Towards a Mythology: Studies in the Poetry of W. B. Yeats*. London, University Press of Liverpool, Hodder & Stoughton Ltd., 1946.

the mood of 'The Second Coming' written some twenty years earlier. And the manner of projecting the prophetic atmosphere is similar in both poems.[1] Each relies on a machinery of questions, in the style of the ancient oracles as we see them described in the poetic riddles of the Greek *Anthology*.[2] In 'The Second Coming' Yeats had climaxed the mood of prescience with the now famous question:

> What rough beast its hour come round at last
> Slouches toward Bethlehem to be born?

And in 'The Statues' the strands are similarly integrated by the urgent demand:

> When Pearse summoned Cuchulain to his side
> What stalked through the Post Office? What intellect,
> What calculation, number, measurement, replied?

When Yeats summons the spirit of the ancient Irish rebel king to the side of Pearse, one of the heroes of the Easter Rebellion in the Dublin Post Office massacre, the imagery (oddly enough, expressed in the *abstract* terms of 'calculation, number, measurement') unites the theme of a great racial memory to the idea of a Pythagorean anonymity. The union of both these themes in a conjunctive question allows Yeats to make the dark prophecy of the last lines, where the Irish are

[1] It can also be profitably compared with 'The Gyres'. See discussion below, pp. 97 ff.

[2] The lines in 'The Second Coming', surely some revelation is at hand; surely the Second Coming is at hand. While declarative in shape are, in emotive intention, interrogative.

seen as the heirs of 'that ancient sect', a phrase ambiguously effective for *either* the Greek sculptors or the ancient Irish heroes, or *both*. The method is powerful. Contrary to what one might expect, instead of weakening the reality of the event reported in the question, to ask 'what' of it persuades us that it really happened, or is now happening. Thus, the only judgment we must make concerns the nature of the action reported. The 'what' raises the mystery, heightens the supernaturalness of the incident described.

The prophecy of the last five lines may seem oracular, but even the sayings of the oracles are open to interpretation. These lines are no exception. What is the 'proper dark' to which Yeats says the Irish climb? Here *A Vision* can help us again. 'After an age of necessity', Yeats wrote there, 'truth, goodness, mechanism, science, democracy, abstraction, peace, comes an age of freedom, fiction, evil, kindred, art, particularity, war. Our age has burned to the socket.' Thus, the Irish are returned to their 'proper dark', the condition out of which a new civilization may develop, a civilization which will once again affirm the anonymous perfection of the 'plummet-measured face' of the Greek authors of 'calculation, number, measurement'.

In short, the 'voice' of this poem, if one remembers that every poetic statement implies a speaker, is that of the sage. That this assumption of responsibility was a deliberate feature of Yeats's technique of persuasion is made clear in *A Vision*. Commenting on the 'spirits' who were dictating it to him, he reports that one said: 'We do nothing singly, every act is done by a

E

number at the same instant.' 'I connect them', Yeats explains, 'with an early conviction of mine, that the creative power of the lyric poet depends upon his accepting some one of a few traditional attitudes, lover, sage, hero, scorner of life.' In the last poems, the attitudes that more and more seemed congenial to him were those of the lover and the sage. We can see him in both guises in the poems we are studying.

That Yeats had, to a singular degree, perfected the technique of persuasion which would make such conventional attitudes exciting is evident in the first line of 'The Statues'. The calm, prophetic certainty of the opening, 'Pythagoras planned it. Why did the people stare?' is masterly. It is so authoritative a beginning that we do not even stop to question the historicity of the event. Instead, we are curious to move along and to discover the nature of that which caused the stares. 'It' implies an antecedent reality which, for all we know, is just a trick of Yeats's magical syntax. Indeed, the rhetorical structure of the whole poem is firmly enunciated by this question which dominates the first stanza. Stanza two enlarges on the surrounding circumstances of this introductory question and provides an intensification of the descriptive material. Stanza three is almost strictly narrative, but a divining voice utters the couplet at its end. The last stanza, as I have already indicated, employs a question to facilitate the prophetic ending.

The first stanza introduces all the themes of the poem. Pythagoras, the Greek mathematician, is viewed as the agent behind Greek sculpture. 'Numbers' is a superb example of the impressive syncope Yeats achieves through metaphor. For it was, in fact, not Pythagoras' 'numbers' that 'moved or seemed to move in marble or in bronze' but rather his *principles* of calculation, measurement, which Yeats takes to be the secret of the Greek sculptor's formal ideal, and which, when clothed in the marble flesh of their handiwork, dramatized the mathematician's thought. But these 'numbers' lacked 'character'. 'Character' is a loaded word in the Yeatsian vocabulary. It means, to begin with, all the varied types of persons possible for the poet to explore through his medium. The young man who shocked his father by defining truth as 'dramatic utterance' at some high pitch of passion was deeply attracted to the study of 'character'. Indeed, the whole early theory of the Mask is a device for ensuring the greatest possible plasticity to the individual personality.

But, later on, Yeats came to see the limitations of this view. In the *Autobiographies* he writes: 'Presently, I was indeed to number character itself among the abstractions.' The adverb is misleading. It was not until his last poems that Yeats could bring himself wholly to abandon this concept of 'character'. We see the concept operative in *A Vision* where the twenty-eight phases of the moon are correlated with twenty-six characterological types, two phases not supporting manifestations of human life. But in 'The Statues' Yeats joins the two concepts so central to his scheme · of human nature: the mathematical anonymity of the Greek statues catch fire from the impassioned subjective desire of 'boys and girls, pale from the imagined love/of solitary beds . . .' exactly as the 'characterless' beauty of Maud Gonne had caught fire from the impassioned desire of the youthful Yeats, 'pale' from the imagined love he had enjoyed with this ideal form. The echoes of Blake's *Visions of the Daughters of Albion* are undeniably powerful:

The moment of desire! The moment of desire! The
  Virgin
That pines for man shall awaken her womb to enormous
  joys
In the secret shadows of her chamber: the youth shut
  up from
The lustful joy shall forget to generate and create an
  enormous image
In the shadows of his curtains and in the folds of his
  silent pillow.

How personally freighted this metaphor of the solitary bed had become for Yeats is evident in a letter to Dorothy Wellesley written at about the time of the composition of this poem.[1] 'I had not a symptom of illness yet I had to take to my bed . . . I felt I was in utter solitude. . . .' It was the frenzy of creative desire (Will) that brought character to the 'plummet-measured' faces of the statues. In the background, moving with subterranean force must have been the myth of Pygmalion and Galetea, as well as the derivative notion Yeats had mentioned to Dorothy Wellesley when he described poets as the 'Lovers' of the Muses. It is

[1] January 28, 1937.

precisely as 'lovers' that the pale boys and girls seek to
fathom the perfection of the ideal and to impress
'character' upon it. The plummet, an instrument for
the precise sounding of depths, suggests the difficulty
of this aspiration. But the real conflagration in this
stanza is contributed by the adjective 'Live'. It leaves
this, like so many other poems of this period, as, in
the end, a poem about *life*. Life, is seen as the energiz-
ing principle whether in the world of action,[1] or in
art, which informs the 'ideal' (here, the statues) and
gives it the authenticity of 'character'.

The second stanza shocks us into new attention with
the cryptic denial:

No! Greater than Pythagoras, for the men

One looks back to the preceding stanza in vain to find
the thing now denied greatness. The word 'great', we
find, is not used at all. We are reduced to guesswork.
But the rhetorical force of the 'No!' followed, as it is,
by the comparative 'greater' makes it clear that there
is a conscious subject in the poet's mind. In effect, he
is saying: 'I said in stanza one that Pythagoras was
responsible for the principles incarnated in the perfection of Greek statues. But now I have changed my
mind. It was not Pythagoras who did this, but rather
the actual artists, 'the men/that with a mallet or a chisel
modelled these/calculations that look but casual
flesh . . .' It was they who 'put down/All Asiatic vague
immensities'. Further, it was the Greek sculptors rather
than the Greek galleys which defeated the Persian

[1] Action, for Yeats, would include dreams.

hordes at Salamis ('the many-headed foam') and who left their values extant in the form of the fixed type of beauty which has dominated European civilization for centuries.

Europe put off that foam when Phidias
Gave women dreams and dreams their looking-glass.

For Yeats 'the many-headed foam' of the invading Persian hosts is a heavily-freighted phrase. Like the New England Transcendentalists and especially Emerson (it was he who called his wife 'Mine Asia'), and, no doubt, drawing upon the same Hegelian fountain-head, Yeats saw Asia as a vast female principle or 'Nature'.[1] While Yeats differed from his predecessors, in an arbitrary and hair-splitting degree, as to *when* the process of civilization effects an 'escape' from Nature, in general, Greek civilization represents a partial escape, Christianity a whole one. But Yeats's sexual cosmology added another condition: A Wheel of the Great Year (a cycle of civilization) 'must be thought of as the *marriage* of symbolic Europe and symbolic Asia, the one begetting upon the other'. More, this union or reconciliation of opposites is explicitly referred to the symbolic agency of Phidian art:

'Then in Phidias Ionic and Doric influences unite . . . and all is transformed by the full moon and all abounds

[1] But, elsewhere, still agreeing with Hegel that Asia is the place where every civilization begins, Yeats adds with a surprising humanism: 'Yet we must hold to what we have that the next civilization may be born, not from a virgin's womb, nor a tomb without a body, not from a void, but of our own rich experience.' *On the Boiler*.

70

and flows. . . . Each age unwinds the thread another age has wound, and it amuses one to remember that before Phidias and his westward moving art, Persia fell, and that when the full moon came round again amid eastward moving thought, and brought Byzantine glory, Rome fell.'

The 'one image', then, which 'crossed the many-headed, (the vast multiplicity of Asia or the East) is that of Phidias. This whole complex of arbitrary associations with which Yeats endowed the civilizations of the East and the West becomes reasonably clear in the last prose work Yeats ever undertook, and which consisted of a series of polemical discussions on matters that caught his interest in relation to poetry. 'On the Boiler', as he called the pamphlet series, provides at least one passage which can serve as a condensed exegesis of 'The Statues':

'There are moments when I am certain that art must once again accept those Greek proportions which carry into plastic art the Pythagorean numbers, those faces which are divine because all there is empty and measured. Europe was not born when Greek galleys defeated the Persian hordes at Salamis, but when the Doric studios sent out those broad-backed marble statues against the multiform, vague expressive Asiatic sea, they gave to the sexual instinct of Europe its goal, its fixed type.'[1]

But for local exegesis, I must return to stanza three.

[1] Mr. Louis MacNeice was the first to point out the fidelity with which these ideas are reflected in 'The Statues'.

The Eastern ideal (composed, as we have seen, of many private strains in Yeats's real-life experience) made concrete in 'a fat/Dreamer of the Middle Ages' is assigned a prescience beyond 'knowledge'. The features of this wisdom are those of Yeats's own boyish observation of the 'empty, staring eyeballs' of the Greek statues at the British Museum. To say (this is another useful example of the way Yeats forces syntax into the service of metaphoric organization) that 'Empty eyeballs knew/that knowledge increases unreality, that/Mirror on mirror mirrored is all the show' is perplexing. Empty eyeballs cannot, of course, logically 'know' anything. But the possessors of empty eyeballs can. Here it is the fat dreamer of the Middle Ages with whose person is fused the mindlessness of the Greek ideal as represented for Yeats in the statues at the British Museum. But while the illusory quality of knowledge (here, Yeats refers again to that 'abstract' knowledge which he despised) is aptly dramatized by the mirror-on-mirror imagery, there is an ironic reservation implied in the following lines:

When gong and conch declare the hour to bless
Grimalkin crawls to Buddha's emptiness.

Here the Easternness of the fused personality who is the 'fat Dreamer' is stressed in such a way that, for the moment, he *becomes* Buddha.[1] We note how subtly

[1] This bringing together into a single unit of meaning seemingly disparate planes of history or civilizations is not only a method, but a value exploited, in varying degrees of thoroughness, by the major literary innovators of this century. If one were

the 'gong' and 'conch' function as dramatic props for underlining the Oriental atmosphere of this bit. But, in the very next line, Grimalkin (the homely, old-English appellation for she-cat), punctures the omni-science attributed to the dreaming, Buddha-like person. Even the visual picture one makes of a cat crawling to the embrace of the divine figure is ludicrous. But closer study suggests that Yeats is specifically rejecting only the institutional, ceremonial aspects of Buddha. The strong end-rhymes of 'bless' and 'emptiness' bear out this supposition. It is as a figure invoked for bless-ing that Buddha is 'empty'. In its other aspects, the Oriental ideal is celebrated for its superior knowledge of 'reality'.[1]

In the last stanza the basic circle of the Pythagoras-statue metaphor is completed. The little peripheral excursions we have discussed have enriched the firm contour of the basic line. The Irish are seen not only as of the lineage of the heroic Cuchulain, but as heirs of the principles of 'calculation, number, measure-ment' of the Greeks.

It is typical of the tortuous processes of Yeats's thinking that he should write a poem in dispraise of

to construct a scale to express this relationship, one might put Yeats, in his later work, at the lowest end of the scale, Eliot, especially in *The Wasteland*, next, with Pound's *Cantos* and Joyce's *Ulysses* and *Finnegans Wake* at the farthest extreme.

[1] A persuasive reading for this section has been supplied by Mr. Robert Linscott. Reality is an illusion and the more we think we know the less we really know. In the same way, at the level of metaphysical speculation, the tenets of all religions from the most primitive (symbolized by the witch's cat) to the most sophisticated (symbolized by Guatama) are empty words.

intellect or 'abstractions' and, in the end, arrive at an endorsement of that which he had thought to despise. These oddly oscillating loyalties wrote such a mercurial line in his work, that, by the time of the difficult late poems, we cannot safely assign any single belief even to a single poem. In 'The Statues', Yeats's ambivalence is memorably traced in the magnificent antithesis of the closing lines. The Irish, wrecked by the 'formless, spawning fury' of 'the filthy modern tide' must 'climb' to their 'proper dark'. The verb is notable. From a more predictable poet we should have expected a verb suggesting descent into or penetration of the 'dark' as the condition of rebirth. Apart from the strong diphthongal emphasis of its vowel, 'climb', in addition, evokes the discipline, effort, or willed action that is involved in such a return to the 'proper' prophetic stature of the Irish.

It is not submission to an inevitable historic pattern that Yeats wants, but a laborious ascent to a previous condition of virtue. The goal is beautifully expressed in the original terms of the poetic analogy: to 'trace the lineaments of a plummet-measured face'. *Trace* here implies both to discern and to draw. The first sense stresses the belief that the Irish must repossess the sources of their ancient power by perception, or insight; the second ties this whole process in with the perennial theme of art, never very far from Yeats's mature interest. Art is now conceived both as a privilege and a responsibility, and is no longer exclusively the possession of the artist. The permissive 'may' helps this sense along. Its power can, as the end-result in a

74

chain of resolute self-exploration, be apprehended in the classic exactitudes of the 'plummet-measured face', just as it had once been Yeats's private vision of the loved contours of Maud Gonne's divinely human one.

A BRONZE HEAD

Here at right of the entrance this bronze head,
Human, superhuman, a bird's round eye,
Everything else withered and mummy-dead.
What great tomb-haunter sweeps the distant sky
(Something may linger there though all else die;)
And finds there nothing to make its terror less
Hysterica passio of its own emptiness?

No dark tomb-haunter once; her form all full
As though with magnanimity of light,
Yet a most gentle woman; who can tell
Which of her forms has shown her substance right?
Or maybe substance can be composite,
Profound McTaggart thought so, and in a breath
A mouthful held the extreme of life and death.

But even at the starting-post, all sleek and new,
I saw the wildness in her and I thought
A vision of terror that it must live through
Had shattered her soul. Propinquity had brought
Imagination to that pitch where it casts out
All that is not itself: I had grown wild
And wandered murmuring everywhere, 'My child,
    my child!'

Or else I thought her supernatural;
As though a sterner eye looked through her eye
On this foul world in its decline and fall;
On gangling stocks grown great, great stocks run
    dry,
Ancestral pearls all pitched into a sty,
Heroic reverie mocked by clown and knave,
And wondered what was left for massacre to save.

2

A BRONZE HEAD

When Dr. Jeffares confidently tells us that a head of Maud Gonne by Lawrence Campbell in the Dublin Municipal Gallery 'inspired this fine poem . . . which left the subject of her human and superhuman qualities and yet again (in an unpublished verse) faced death triumphantly' we may be deceived into thinking that this biographical location illumines the poem's rich darkness. But once we have reminded ourselves of Yeats's dismay at the 'old bellows full of angry wind' which Maud, along with other beautiful and intellectual women, seemed to have become; of his earlier belief in the power of beautiful women to transcend ordinary experience, become 'supernatural', in his peculiar use of that word; of Yeats's mention of *Hysterico passio* in *A Vision*, what do we have to make the poem more accessible to the reader?

The question I want to consider is whether by systematically following the signposts provided by the poem *itself* we shall discern a self-contained unit of experience, that thing which, at some level, every work of art must be. Let us assume, for experiment's sake, a fictitious 'innocence', one which I have earlier deemed an expensive habit for the critic to don, and consider the poem, for the moment, as a verbal "objet trouvé"

with its own mysterious density and oneness. To this
end, the opening words are useful:

> Here at the right of the entrance this bronze head
> Human, superhuman, bird's round eye,
> Everything else withered and mummy-dead.

Where are we? In a tomb? How are we to guess this is
the Dublin Municipal Gallery did we not have access
to that adventitious bit of information? But does it
really matter whether we ever know this fact or not?
I do not think so. Everything in the décor of these lines
is tomb-like. The bronze head is the head of someone
no longer alive. Only the eye has power; everything
else pertaining to it has withered, is 'mummy-dead'.
The eye, round and staring, that convention in statuary
which, as we have seen, so impressed Yeats, is like
the eye of 'master Caesar' in a poem of the same period,[1]
'fixed on nothing'. But the head is human, even superhuman, although everything else once associated with
it is dead. Yet it is possible that the spirit of this dead
thing, may preserve something of itself—though all
else die—and persist as a 'great tomb-haunter'. But the
nature of spirit ('tomb-haunter' is significant) is such
that it finds not consolation for its terror, only the
hysterical mockery of its own emptiness. While it is
interesting to know of Yeats's belief, derived from
Eastern mysticism, that the spirit of the dead relive
their past and suffer, at least for a while, a purgatorial
re-enactment of their agonies, this does not greatly en-

[1] 'Long-Legged Fly'.

hance the direct statement of the lines as they stand on the page.

As so often in Yeats's oddly argumentative poetic dialectic, the tone of his case changes with the very first words of the next stanza, which further describe the *living* past of the now-dead person. It is a female person, who not only was 'No dark tomb-haunter once' but, to the contrary, 'a form all full of light'. The accents of the describing voice are now warm and softened. The lovely Shakespearean cadence of 'Yet a most gentle woman' balances the rhetorical force of the argument by a parallel placement of the caesura with that of 'No dark tomb-haunter once'. Because of this placement, both 'once' and 'woman' inherit a falling, nostalgic accent. But, as in stanza one, the argument is deflected by a question and the stanza ends with that formal shape, but now without the helping question-mark. The question is: is it the conception of the woman as a 'dark tomb-haunter' or as alive with the 'magnanimity of light' which most reveals her 'substance'? Under which aspect can we re-possess the real person, or is substance 'composite'? (Yeats, I should guess, pronounced 'composite' with the accent on the first syllable and to rhyme with 'right'. I have heard old English people pronounce 'opposite' similarly.)

We need not identify McTaggart as the philosopher who wrote the *Studies in Hegelian Cosmology* which Yeats had read in 1928. It is enough for the poetic intention to know that he was someone Yeats deemed 'profound' and one who held significant views about life and death. The introduction of his commonplace name into

the body of this most 'rich, dark' poem is a master-
stroke of strategy. It is a spike of everydayness which
relieves the sombre décor and confers a kind of daylight sensibleness on the inquiry. McTaggart's view (at
least as Yeats presents it) is the familiar paradox of
death-in-life and life-in-death which Yeats, along with
other poets in an honourable tradition going back to
Heraclitus, movingly explored.

The opening 'But' of stanza three shows Yeats using
a favourite device of this period. It hastens the argument along *as if* some other avenue of speculation were
being opened. For the moment, this does indeed happen. But we shall see that we are led back, in the end,
to where we started. Now we see the woman in her
youth as a runner in a race, as a young colt 'all sleek
and new'. Even then the poet sensed she was possessed
by a terror of her own destiny. The next lines are
memorable:

> . . . Propinquity had brought
> Imagination to that pitch where it casts out
> All that is not itself. . . .

The most obvious reference is to Yeats's long and
unsatisfactory passion for Maud Gonne. But that
hardly provides a gloss. The situation Yeats describes
is a more universal predicament. It results from that
intensity which a long association of values breeds in
the mind so that eventually certain concerns become
obsessive: 'imagination casts out all that is not itself . . .'
Once again from the kernel of a particular, concrete
fixation (Maud) Yeats can so generalize the operations

of the mind that the experience provokes a shock of recognition from us all. But the process is incomplete: once the compulsive value takes such feverish possession of the mind, the whole man, too, grows 'wild'. The touching confession,

> And wandered murmuring everywhere, 'My
> child, my child!'

is the completion of this brilliant merger of the particular and the general. When the mind is so dominated and so teeming with its own creatures, the condition becomes valued as a thing-in-itself, as integral to personality, because created from the self, like a child.

But even this aspect of Maud does not exhaust her richness as a symbol. The opening disjunction of the next stanza allows Yeats to expand the flow of his argument into yet another branch of possibility:

> Or else I thought her supernatural;
> As though a sterner eye looked through her eye
> On this foul world in its decline and fall;

Now we need not quibble over the private associations Yeats conferred on 'supernatural'. Nor need we worry about its frequent appearance in other poems. Here the context makes the immediate usage perfectly clear:[1] the woman was once thought to be the agent of a *judging* principle which was not human but eternal.

[1] In *A Vision* Yeats's peculiar use of 'supernatural' is illumined by the following passage which makes it clear he meant it not so much as 'spiritual' or 'above the natural', but as 'ideal'. 'In the completely primary or completely antithetical state there is only a supernatural or ideal existence.'

As such, she was felt to condemn the quality of modern experience with 'gangling stocks grown great' (the rise of the middle classes), 'great stocks run dry' (the decline of the aristocracy) and 'Heroic reverie mocked by clown and knave' (the rejection of poetry, especially the form favoured by Yeats—dramatic soliloquy in verse drama). All these are, of course, the poet's own beliefs projected into the woman. But, let us note, it is 'the sterner eye' looking through her eye which is the subject of the last terrifying line:

And wondered what was left for massacre to save.

This is the powerful theme of rebirth through violent destruction which Yeats had uttered in such a memorable voice in 'The Second Coming' and 'Byzantium'. It is true that this conception of 'the crime of birth, the pain of death' is expounded in *A Vision*. But it is not peculiar to Yeats's cosmology, being a familiar paradox not only in the philosophic thought of antiquity, but in the vocabulary of modern psycho-analytic theory as well. The 'birth-trauma' and the 'death-wish' are reasonably close approximations to the Yeatsian formulation.

In an early version of the poem[1] there is an additional stanza. Its deletion from the published version is significant:

O Hour of triumph, come and make me gay.
If burnished chariots are put to flight
Why brood on old triumph: prepare to die.
Even at the approach of un-imaged night

[1] Printed by Dr. Jeffares, op. cit., p. 297.

Man has the refuge of his gaiety.
A dab of black enhances every white.
Tension is but the rigour of the mind
Canon the god and father of mankind.

It was sound to cast out this stanza, apart from any purely textural adequacy it may have (I think it less taut than the other stanzas) for it shifts the focus of interest from the bronze head to the singer himself and introduces a blatantly *didactic* direction to a poem whose essential shape is a question. It is a question which, like many others, was left significantly unanswered by Yeats. No doubt the whole fiction of the bronze head may be taken as a convenient mould for Yeats to throw his questions into. But the deleted stanza would, inevitably, have over-weighted this intention.

On the technical side, it is interesting to add to those matters of the first importance which we have already noted, the fact that Yeats was drawing sustenance from his re-reading of Shakespeare at about this time,[1] and especially from the Shakespeare of the sonnets and the early plays. I have already mentioned the import of the caesura in lines one and three of this poem, and now point to the Shakespearean echoes (to say nothing of Gibbon!) in the line

On this foul world in its decline and fall.

Because the closing lines of the end-couplets in stanzas three and four are lengthened into alexandrines, their powerful delivery is heightened.

[1] 1934–5.

For the rest, the shadowy woman who is immortalized in 'A Bronze Head' can be usefully seen against the character of Emer in the play, *The Only Jealousy of Emer*, written almost twenty years before. Emer's beauty, too, Mr. Ure notes, has been planned by Pythagoras and shows 'The lineaments of a plummet-measured face'. Her tragedy is that all men will love her but

> He that has loved the best
> May turn from a statue
> His too human breast.

The popular metaphoric use of 'statue' in the passage above, a use which in everyday speech stresses the cold, lifeless aspects of personality, points the irony with which Yeats now invested the image of Maud Gonne. But while these lines are richly eloquent of Yeats's personal relations with Maud, by the time of the composition of 'A Bronze Head' his attitude to her had undergone considerable intellectual refinement. The basic comparison of Maud to a rigid inhuman object is perpetuated, and even helped, by the literal coincidence of having the actual bronze head at hand. Nevertheless, Maud is now seen as the agency for a power that may be beyond her control. The bitterness has burned itself away.

The most we can say, then, as we conclude our study of this poem, to the suggestion that to know any one of the later poems, it is necessary to know all of Yeats, is this: while it is true that the poet projects some of his own favourite theories into the dramatic effigy

86

of Maud Gonne as a bronze head, these ideas can be got just as successfully from the poem, although in different terms, than from any other source. Whenever possible, in critical reading, we must put our faith in the poem, letting *it* do the work for us, rather than relying on the risky props of biography, history, psychology, or 'philosophy'. The 'philosophy', if any, to be found in a poem by Yeats, or any good poet for that matter, had better be called something else if we do not wish to confuse inextricably our universes of discourse.

GROUP THREE

1. THE GYRES

2. THE MAN AND THE ECHO

THE GYRES

The gyres! the gyres! Old Rocky Face, look forth;
Things thought too long can be no longer thought,
For beauty dies of beauty, worth of worth,
And ancient lineaments are blotted out.
Irrational streams of blood are staining earth;
Empedocles has thrown all things about;
Hector is dead and there's a light in Troy;
We that look on but laugh in tragic joy.

What matter though numb nightmare ride on top,
And blood and mire the sensitive body stain?
What matter? Heave no sigh, let no tear drop,
A greater, a more gracious time has gone;
For painted forms or boxes of make-up
In ancient tombs I sighed, but not again;
What matter? Out of cavern comes a voice,
And all it knows is that one word 'Rejoice!'

Conduct and work grow coarse, and coarse the soul,
What matter? Those that Rocky Face holds dear,
Lovers of horses and of women, shall,
From marble of a broken sepulchre,
Or dark betwixt the polecat and the owl,
Or any rich, dark nothing disinter
The workman, noble and saint, and all things run
On that unfashionable gyre again.

I

THE GYRES

'The Gyres', alone of the *Last Poems*, has received some critical attention from a number of Yeats's biographers and critics. The reason for this is clear. It connects easily with several earlier poems, such as 'The Second Coming' and 'The Tower', because of its basic gyral imagery. More, *A Vision* proves very helpful with exegesis, and provides a fund of extra-poetic material which can be woven in to elucidate the poem. Richard Ellman, for example, is interested in the gyres as the symbolic centre of Yeats's cosmology and, while he barely mentions the poem, devotes considerable space in his book to diagrams of the gyres, and their supposed source, Solomon's seal. Professor Stauffer, in the study I have referred to, does some reliable tracking down of uses of the word 'gyre' in the body of Yeats's poems but then goes on to the questionable generalization: 'Opposed to ganglions that suggest intellect, art and age, symbolized by the gyre and stone, are ganglions that suggest passion, life and youth, symbolized by the sea and animal blood.' Not only, as will be seen in our analysis of 'The Gyres', is the linking of gyre and stone a mésalliance, but the actual equivalents which Mr. Stauffer assigns them—'intellect, art and age'—betray a fatal insensitivity to how the creative mind works in poetry. His description of the *use* of 'gyres' in the poem of that name adds little to our knowledge or our pleasure. Now, if we can assign any *general* use to the word 'gyre' in the Yeatsian vocabulary, or, rather, find any *common* element which it carries in different contexts, it would be something like this: The interlocking gyres represent process; they are the characteristic movement or dynamic of the universe. As such, they explain the career of individual human experience, as well as that of civilizations and universes.

Dr. Jeffares's brief analysis of this poem is equally based on the ideas of *A Vision*, and is, although perhaps not only for this reason, equally unsatisfactory. While he quite reasonably suggests that the gyres depict the cycle of change described in *A Vision*, his analysis of the features of the poem which gets no elucidation from the prose work, invalidates the body of his criticism. First, the poem does not, as Dr. Jeffares states, open by apostrophizing the gyres. To point to, as in the opening exclamation, 'The gyres! the gyres!' is not the same as to apostrophize. What follows is even more curious. 'Old Rocky Face', says Dr. Jeffares, 'is Shelley's Jew who lived in a cavern amid the Demonesi'[1]. Not at all. This frivolous importation adds nothing to the poem and it is significant that Dr. Jeffares does not tell us why Shelley's Jew should participate in it.

---

[1] Professor Stauffer is equally (although not as irrelevantly) off the track. Of Old Rocky Face he asks: 'What do we have here? The Sphinx-like beast of 'The Second Coming', or memories of native Irish mountains, Ben Bulben perhaps, which Yeats associated with supernatural happenings?'

I hope I shall not be thought carping for the foregoing remarks. My real point is not a petty one. It is that the mere tracking down of sources, even if the critic happens to get the right one, is not an organic way to explore imagery. Even should the critic locate the right source for a particular symbol, he still hasn't told us why *it*, rather than some other detail of the poet's experience, was incorporated into the special affective complex which the poem is. There is an embarassing mechanicality evident in Dr. Jeffares's further attempts to employ what he must conceive as the approach of the 'new' criticism: 'There is an inhuman remoteness from ordinary life in the poem with its insistence achieved by a repetition of key words: 'The gyres! the gyres! For beauty dies of beauty, worth of worth', 'What matter? [repeated four times] . . .'.

I should like to preface what I consider a relevant, although certainly not an exclusive, reading of this difficult poem by a few general remarks which have a bearing on it. Back in the nineties, Yeats may have been struck by the word 'gyre' in a poem of Francis Thompson's which evidently made a deep impression on him for he quotes it thirty years later in *A Vision*. The subject-matter of the quoted passage is, moreover, remarkably close to the main idea of Yeats's 'system' as set down in *A Vision*:

Not only of cyclic Man
Thou here discern'st the plan,
Not only of cyclic Man, but of the cyclic Me
Not only of Immortalities great years

The reflex just appears
But thine own bosom's year, still circling round
In ample and in ampler gyre
Towards the far completion, wherewith crowned
Love unconsumed shall chant on his own funeral
pyre.

Perhaps the earliest use of 'gyre' in Yeats's own poetry was in the superb opening of 'The Second Coming', written in 1919:

Turning and turning in the widening gyre
The falcon cannot hear the falconer;

Related poems of the same period turn up a frequent use of the word,[1] and it continues to appear in some of the best poems of the following decade,[2] until by 1935, the probable date of the composition of 'The Gyres', the gyres themselves become the subject-matter of the poem.

We can trace, then, how Thompson's conjunction of the gyre symbol with his notion of 'cyclic Man' had, by the time of the writing of *A Vision* in the early twenties, taken on a deepened meaning for Yeats. It was in 1929 that he wrote from Shillingford to his friend, Mrs. Shakespear, that he was searching out signs of the whirling gyres of the historical cones in occult books such as Mrs. Strong's *Apotheosis and After-Life*, and that by studying them he hoped to see deeper into what was to come. 'My own pilosophy', he added,

[1] See 'Demon and Beast' and 'Shepherd and Goatherd'.
[2] See 'All Soul's Night' and 'Byzantium'.

'does not much brighten the prospect so far as any future we shall live.' By the time of the composition of 'The Gyres' fourteen years later, his pessimism was even more profound. And, significantly, it is at about this time that in his letters to Dorothy Wellesley Yeats talks of the spirits of the dead in folklore who are represented as being enveloped in a whirlwind. This whirling metaphor is expanded in 'The Gyres' to embrace the cyclic movement of history which includes not only the spirits of the dead, but dead cultures and civilizations as well.

And, if we must further unravel the complex web of associations which the symbol of the gyre carried for Yeats, there are many useful passages in *A Vision*, which point to the common element present in *all* the uses of the word which I have indicated. Thus, for example, in the amusing faked introduction to that alleged mystical book of the sixteenth century, Yeats wrote:

'The anguish of birth and death cry out in the same instant. Life is no series of emanations from divine reason such as the Cabalists imagine, but an irrational bitterness, no orderly descent from level to level, no waterfall but a whirlpool, a gyre.'

Later, Yeats attempts to trace various mentions of gyres in antiquity, through Aquinas and up to Swedenborg. All these 'historical' gyres appear to share two elements in common: circular movement and a combination of two opposite movements. Without detaining ourselves to expound the questionable structure of

Yeats's 'system', it is nevertheless important to understand that he sees his cones and gyres as the *principles* of energy which move the Four Faculties, and which generate the patterns of their movements. I do not think that anyone has pointed out that this creative antagonism of opposites which Yeats makes the axis of his cosmology is really an extension of his early and presumably abandoned theory of the Mask, a theory originally centred in the value of conflict to the creative imagination, but now universalized into a dynamic principle which accounts for both human and superhuman growth. That the early version of this belief was unconsciously working towards its later enlargement is indicated by a revealing passage in 'The Trembling of the Veil', the section of Yeats's *Autobiographies* which deals with the years between 1887 and 1891:

'My mind began drifting vaguely towards the doctrine of "the mask" which convinced me that ever-passionate man . . . is, as it were, linked with another age historical or imaginary, where he alone finds images that rouse his energy.'

Now, while these symbolic analogues of Yeats are often arbitrary, unclear, and even absurd, they must be regarded as the efforts of a rich but unsophisticated mind to work out an ethos and a psychology that would order its multiple and perplexing experience. Oddly enough, Yeats was sufficiently given over to a long habit of introspection about his own thought-processes to be aware of this. He had written to his father just before his marriage in 1917 that he was working out a religious system which was helping his verse by giving him a 'framework of patterns'. And the profound intellectual therapy of this effort—'getting the disorder of one's mind in order'—Yeats put as co-evalent with 'the real impulse to create'.

Before I attempt to weight the 'philosophic' gravity of 'The Gyres' as an expression of the will-to-order which Yeats equated with the poetic function, I should like to make a technical study of its construction. And I do not for a moment suggest that such an inspection is incidental to the other end. On the contrary, if there is a 'philosophic' import to be got from the poem, this is the only way I know to get at it. For we can then feel confident that the 'philosophy' has been precipitated by the *facts* of the poem, rather than by our secondary sources of knowledge concerning Yeats's beliefs.

The opening injunction of 'The Gyres' is unambiguous:

The gyres! the gyres! Old Rocky Face, look forth;
Things thought too long can be no longer thought.

The gyres, a cosmic phenomenon, are pointed to as event, much as one would call attention to a comet trailing the sky. It is Old Rocky Face who is enjoined to watch. Old Rocky Face is the poet, wearing a very transparent mask. It is he, Yeats, who is old, rocky; it is he, Yeats (stanza two) who is the 'lover of horses and women' and not Shelley's Jew. And the voice that is calling Rocky Face is that 'antithetical self', the poet in his other, prophetic guise. This conclusion is supported by the many poems of the last phase written in the form

99

of an interior dialogue. 'The Man and the Echo', which we shall study as a companion piece to this poem, employs an objective dialogue structure; the voice of 'The Gyres' is a single one which, by a narrative rhetoric, talks for the suppressed aspect of the self here called 'Old Rocky Face'. A dialogue of the self and the anti-self, 'Ego Dominus Tuus', written in 1915, shows how early this strategy of dramatizing the conflicts of personality by splitting off the warring elements into fictive personae suggested itself to Yeats. Excitingly, it is in this very poem, written two decades before 'The Gyres' that we find an image which is the prototype of Rocky Face: the reference is to Dante:

> I think he fashioned from his opposite
> An image that might have been a stony face.

By the time Yeats comes to write 'The Gyres' and 'The Man and the Echo', it is himself he sees as the stony face. In a draft of the latter poem which he enclosed in a note to Dorothy Wellesley, the Man addresses the Echo as 'O rocky void'. In the printed version it becomes—and the capitals are significant— 'O Rocky Voice'. This is the poet addressing his anti-self, Echo. 'Rocky Face' in 'The Gyres' is the identical element in his personality, but deprived of his speaking voice. In this connection it is interesting to note that both poems are alike indebted to a cavern or tomb atmosphere. And, if we must bring Shelley in, it might better be in the distinction Yeats had made in 1900 between his symbols of tower and cave: 'The contrast between it (the tower) and the cave', he had written,

'. . . suggests a contrast between the mind looking outward upon men and things and the mind looking inward upon itself. . . .' Yeats adds that these associations
may or may not have been in Shelley's mind. Certainly
they existed in his own.

The pervasiveness of the tower symbol in the poetry
of the twenties—significantly, the first decade of his
marriage—when Yeats appeared to be at last achieving
a relatively outward adjustment, is to be contrasted with
the epithets of the thirties, the Rocky Voices, and the
Rocky Faces. The conclusion is inevitable and almost
every one of the *Last Poems* tends to urge it: the closing
years of his life threw Yeats back upon his introspec-
tive habit with an additional intensity possibly effected
by the temporary revitalization of sexuality. Thus, it
was with a more troubled consciousness of the complexity of this process of 'the mind looking inward
upon itself' that these poems were written. They were,
moreover, a description of the *action* of this process
itself.

The fiction of 'The Gyres', then, is the fiction of the
split person. And the ecstatic voice which urges Old
Rocky Face to 'look forth' is the voice of Yeats's other
self. I have mentioned Dr. Jeffares's list of 'key-words',
but of these I can only accept 'gyres' as a true one. For
if the whole notion of 'key-words' is not to become
another mechanical short-cut in the reading of poetry,
it must be reserved for those words about which cluster
the emotional centres of the poem. The mere fact of the
repetition of a word does not in itself, as Dr. Jeffares and
some others appear to suppose, constitute a key-word.

On the foregoing definition, I should add to 'gyres', as genuine key-words, 'blood', 'stain', and 'cavern'. But if my own series is to stand as a more than arbitrary choice, it must be elucidated.

'Blood' is central to stanza one and, at a reduced intensity, to stanza two. The total atmosphere of the first stanza is one of destruction, chaos, and terror. Against this is put the great cyclic energy of the gyres, which, as they whirl away the memory of the ancient lineaments, and refine away the vitality of an unreplenished art and morality, foreshadow, if by no other means than the exclamation points which announce them, some kind of positive deliverance.

'Stain', while a true key-word, does not work solely by its own power but in conjunction with 'blood'. 'The irrational streams of blood . . . Staining earth' point to a cosmic cataclysm. Stanza two narrows this holocaust to a statement of the individual's dishonour: 'And blood and mire the sensitive body stain', thus permitting the poet to speak in his own voice in the lines:

> For painted forms or boxes of make-up
> In ancient tombs I sighed, but not again;

Phonetically, both 'blood' and 'stain' are strong words. In addition, they are so positioned that they inherit the metrical emphasis of the line.

'Cavern' is a less obvious key-word. In a later poem, 'Those Images', one of the most balanced, healthy, and ideologically clear of the *Last Poems*, the Mind is told to leave its 'caverns' for

There's better exercise
In the sunlight and wind.[1]

In 'The Gyres', 'cavern' is used only once and its position is not as distinctive metrically as those of the keywords we have just looked at. But it re-enforces, and indeed, is a *part of* the symbol of 'Old Rocky Face', an epithet for those elements in the self which Yeats associates with the congealed areas of personality, 'Things thought too long can be no longer thought'. In addition, the 'cavern' represents that layer of personality most inaccessible to consciousness, but which yet increases itself by this neglect, pushing its way into the conscious mind and there dictating its demands seemingly 'against' reason.[2]

But the cavern metaphor serves Yeats at yet another level of argument in *A Vision* where it is a kind of metaphysical archetype. In one of the strangest passages in that dubious concoction, Yeats wrote:

'At or near the central point of a lunar month of classical civilization . . . came the Christian primary dispensation, the child born in the Cavern. At or near the central point of our civilization must come antithetical revelation, the turbulent child of the Altar.'

[1] I cannot resist the temptation to point out how Yeats repeats the triumph of 'A Coat':

> 'For there's more enterprise
> In walking naked,'

in a poem written some thirty years later and with equal success.

[2] There is no great distinction between this conception and the Freudian 'unconscious'.

103

The womb analogy of 'Cavern' in this passage connects suggestively with its use in 'The Gyres'. There it is the subconscious areas of personality which give birth to the commands put upon the conscious intellect. Yeats, in the passage above, appends a curious footnote. While I am not certain that it adds much to the cavern metaphor, it nevertheless has a peripheral use in demonstrating how arbitrarily Yeats picked up material which became highly charged with symbolic meaning and spread out in ever-widening circles into the texture of his thought and work. 'I am thinking', he says, 'of two symbols found by Frobenius in Africa, the Cavern, symbol of the nations moving westward, the Altar at the centre of radiating roads, symbol of the nations, moving eastwards.' While, apparently insensitive to the naïveté of this attempt to describe the movements of cultures, Yeats puts forward his own position unambiguously, if unscientifically: 'I, upon the other hand, must think all civilizations equal at their best; every phase returns, therefore in some sense every civilization.' This belief, like many others Yeats held on allied subjects at this time, is taken over almost in its entirety from Flinders Petrie's, *The Revolution of Civilizations* and F. von Hügel's, *The Mystical Element of Religion*.[1]

[1] Petrie, the great nineteenth-century archeologist, and von Hügel, the historian of mystical thought, shared some ideas, although whether the two influenced one another is neither within my interests nor my competency to ascertain. In any event, they apparently appealed to Yeats for similar reasons. In von Hügel, Yeats found an eruditely argued thesis regarding the impact of mystical experience on spiritual life. Von Hügel, as early as 1908, was trying to revive Kierkegaard. Yeats also found in von Hügel

The deep subsconscious impulses welling up from the 'cavern' check the denying intellect which has renounced the 'painted forms and boxes of make-up' sought in ancient tombs. The materials of the latter image are almost certainly derived from Yeats's early study of occult symbols as well as the cabalistic exercises and charts of the Hermetic students and Madame

an attractively simple, if naïve scheme to account for the character of Western culture.

But it was von Hügel's conclusion which proved most congenial to Yeats for it squared with his own assessment. Von Hügel wrote that it was 'only through self-renunciation and suffering that the soul can win its true self, its abiding joy in union with the source of life . . . and the choice between two things alone: the noble pangs of spiritual childbirth, of painful joyous expansion and growth; and the shameful ache of spiritual death, of dreary contraction and decay.'

In Petrie's *The Revolutions of Civilizations* (1911), Yeats found a metaphor which he took over as a *principle* in his own description of the revolutions of civilizations. Petrie employs the concept behind the 'Great Year' of the ancients, but he is careful to point out that this is merely a metaphor based on the natural cycle of summer and winter which has come to stand for the decline and fall of civilizations. Being an archeologist, Petrie takes sculpture as the test of the strength of a civilization, a concept which we see Yeats borrows in 'The Statues'.

One suspects that the most influential features of Petrie's thought for Yeats was his dread of democracy which he sees as 'the regular feature of decaying civilizations', and his belief that the condition of a civilization's continuance demands strife. 'There is no advance without strife.' Unlike Yeats, however, Petrie looks to the future with a great surge of inherited nineteenth-century optimism. The verse-play, 'A Full Moon in March', is interesting, among other reasons, for its reflection of some of Petrie's ideas. See, for example, the lines:

> Great nations blossom above
> A slave bows down to a slave.

Blavatsky's theosophical group. Intuition or impulse contradicts the renouncing intellect with the imperative 'Rejoice!' This reading of the second stanza is substantiated by the heavy ironical intonation of 'What matter?' coming after the resolve to give up the fruitless sighs for an impossible past. The fact that the question is separated from 'not again' only by a semicolon, which does not effectively end-stop the line, shows that Yeats meant it as a mocking echo, an involuntary negation of the weak resolve.

'A greater, a more gracious time has gone' represents a conclusion Yeats had reached at as far back as 1909 when he had written in his diary that to oppose the new ill-breeding of Ireland, 'I can set up a secondary or interior personality, created out of the tradition of myself and this personality (alas, only possible to me in my writing) must be always gracious and simple. . . '. What qualities he attached to these adjectives is further intimated when he added 'A great lady is as simple as a good poet'.

In 'The Gyres' Yeats is in effect abandoning personal responsibility for making a reality of such graciousness '. . . I sighed, but not again'; and putting all the intensity of his wilful old heart into the gyres, those principles of the revolutions of cultures which would restore from the sepulchre certain aspects of the past which he had always connected with 'graciousness'. But in the twenties, let us say, Yeats would have assigned more power to the men of action, the 'lovers of horses and of women', whom he still held dear. Now, he sees them in the service of the gyrating cones

106

of history and as auxiliary forces which, together with these cyclic processes, will contrive a return to the conditions he requires for 'Unity of Being'.

Another mark of the subtlety of the Yeatsian vocabulary is to be seen in the use of 'noble' in this same stanza. An overworked adjective in nineteenth-century poetry, it is entirely unobjectionable here because used as a noun. In this archaic sense it operates as co-evalent with 'workman' and 'saint' and seems to restore an original moral lustre to the persons it denotes, a lustre which we should not so readily credit to the 'nobility'.

By the time we reach the 'What matter?' of the last stanza, the phrase has become so charged with scorn and derision that it forces an answer. In this truly apocalyptic passage Rocky Face is told that all the things he values will 'run on that unfashionable gyre again'. 'The dark betwixt the polecat and the owl' is the source from which the new-old order will spring.[1] It is typical of Yeats's method that he saw no contradiction between the 'irrational streams of blood' as defiling earth and man, and the same instinctual sources ('rich, dark nothing') as generating the new cycle of fulfilment.

It is the word 'unfashionable' in the last line of the poem which suggests both irony and self-criticism. For Yeats must have known that his mystical 'gyres' were 'unfashionable'—and in a double sense. They were intellectually unfashionable as an explanation of the

---

[1] See *A Vision* where Phase One is described as 'not being human'. See also the poem 'Phases of the Moon' for further elucidation of the 'ideas' of this passage.

movement of cultures; this particular gyre was politically unfashionable in a scientific, democratic society. For his motive, 'unfashionable' is a magnificent choice, the only sophisticated word in the whole poem, and by its prose quality setting the poem in time and robbing it a little of its gnomic intensity. Thus, it is really an expository short-cut and, while helpful, reduces rather than heightens the spontaneity of the prophecy. That this was a deliberately contrived effect I have no doubt. For Yeats would be the first to know that we have not now the ears with which to hear a 'pure' mantic intonation.

This is a suitable point at which to raise a few questions about the nexus of values—I am careful not to say 'philosophy'—raised by this poem. One consideration, which I hope may in part be answered by the technical study we have just made, is why Yeats's prophecy of a condition in society that many of us should hardly care for seems a desirable even a good thing within the framework of the poem. The frequency with which similar questions crop up in the reading of modern poetry shows how crucial it is to much poetic organization in an age of rival and pluralistic values. Mr. Eliot's very interesting statement on the nature of poetic belief, which I have borrowed as epigraph to this study, does not seem to me enough; or, more precisely, while it may be a description of something that does happen when we read a poem, it is not a description of the *whole* thing that happens. The statement that we learn what it *feels* like for the poet to

believe something does not help us to understand why, when we read the poems of Eliot, Yeats or Pound, we accept beliefs we would not entertain if they were committed to prose statements. If someone will say that Yeats's gyres, Pound's mystique of 'usury', and Eliot's Anglo-Catholicism are merely fictions which the imagination accommodates in the same way it can accommodate unicorns or griffins, I must point out that there seems to me a very real sense in which we must distinguish the plastic sense of the possible which is called up by unicorns and griffins, and the logical sense of the impossible when confronted by gyres, Social Credit, or Anglo-Catholicism.

Now I want to examine, as an approach to this problem, the particular condition of Unity of Being which Yeats is hailing in 'The Gyres', a condition which is to be repossessed by man through the liberating deliverance of the gyres. The Unity of Being which Yeats yearned for had occurred before, sometime around 1450, he wrote in *The Tragic Generation*, although in some parts of Europe a hundred years earlier or later. In this phase and, I should like to point out, significantly, men attained to personality in great numbers and became like 'a perfectly proportioned human body'. Later, Yeats confesses, he saw this dream of his early manhood to be false, and that no modern nation could return to a Unity of Culture, 'though it may be we can achieve it for some small circle of men and women and there leave it till the moon brings round its century'. But we see Yeats reversing this position in 'The Gyres' and taking an oracular stance to prophesy exactly such

a rotation of the gyres that the moon does bring 'round its century' of Unity of Culture, when 'workman, noble, and saint', the three symbolic orders of Unity of Being, would once again dominate the human landscape.

While capitalized abstractions such as the above are calculated to put off the cautious reader, if we were to substitute for Yeats's mystagogical 'Unity of Being' the psychologist's 'integration of personality', the concept seems more acceptable, even if we do not admire the features which Yeats assigns to it. That, it seems to me, is an aspect of the persuasive logic of Yeats's scientific illogicality we need to understand. It is that, the moment we try to assess his naïve and homespun pseudo-philosophical terminology by substituting more neutral terms, the referents of event, situation and attitude in the observable public world often agree with our own experience. More importantly, and this is not to differentiate but to continue my argument, there is much, even at the level of abstraction, that we *can* give our assent to in Yeats's judgment of our moral predicament as he exhibits it within the compelling emotional orbit of the poem. Thus, we move along to the final utterance which climaxes the diagnosis without our questioning—at *that* moment the desirability of the condition it invokes. Dr. B. Rajan, while allowing too much to Yeats's 'system' ('. . . it *explains* more than science does', he writes, 'and *explains* it more poetically'),[1] does

---

[1] 'W. B. Yeats and the Unity of Being', in *The Nineteenth Century*, September, 1949. But to assert is not to explain. Yeats merely asserts.

see, with considerable clarity, the pressures Yeats laboured under:

'The problem of the poet in society—of his inability to redeem or celebrate a system emptied of imaginative meaning—is difficult enough and torturing enough to lead to fanatical and desperate solutions. It is Yeats's achievement to have compelled us to see this breach so plainly. . . . No critic since Matthew Arnold has seen the necessities of his time more clearly, or isolated with more revealing starkness the alienation of the contemporary poet from the prevailing standards and culture of his age.'

But even this generous version of the task Yeats performs in his poetry is not enough, for it does not help us to see how we, the readers who may not be poets, feel so readily involved in the problem. The truth of the matter is that the breach Yeats saw is one which threatens to engulf all of us who, in the first place, become sensitive to its existence. The miracle of Yeats's and of all great art is that out of so personal a vision the artist can compel an assent to a problem which he is the first to pose in exactly those terms. We may not give anything for Yeats's backward looking solutions; that is not to the point. The experience of the poem has shaken us; and we are, in some measure, *changed* by our temporary submission to its tragic and desperate atmosphere. We have looked into the chasm.

THE MAN AND THE ECHO

MAN

In a cleft that's christened Alt
Under broken stone I halt
At the bottom of a pit
That broad noon has never lit,
And shout a secret to the stone.
All that I have said and done,
Now that I am old and ill,
Turns into a question till
I lie awake night after night
And never get the answers right.
Did that play of mine send out
Certain men the English shot?
Did words of mine put too great strain
On that woman's reeling brain?
Could my spoken words have checked
That whereby a house lay wrecked?
And all seems evil until I
Sleepless would lie down and die.

ECHO

Lie down and die.

MAN

That were to shirk
The spiritual intellect's great work,

And shirk it in vain. There is no release
In a bodkin or disease,
Nor can there be work so great
As that which cleans man's dirty slate.
While man can still his body keep
Wine or love drug him to sleep,
Waking he thanks the Lord that he
Has body and its stupidity,
But body gone he sleeps no more,
And till his intellect grows sure
That all's arranged in one clear view,
Pursues the thoughts that I pursue,
Then stands in judgment on his soul,
And, all work done, dismisses all
Out of intellect and sight
And sinks at last into the night.

ECHO

Into the night.

MAN

O Rocky Voice,
Shall we in that great night rejoice?
What do we know but that we face
One another in this place?
But hush, for I have lost the theme,
Its joy or night seem but a dream;
Up there some hawk or owl has struck,
Dropping out of sky or rock,
A stricken rabbit is crying out,
And its cry distracts my thought.

114

2

THE MAN AND THE ECHO

As we have seen, the early version of this poem helps us to read 'The Gyres'. Similarly, the published poems re-enforce one another thematically although the tone of 'The Man and the Echo' is less hortatory. Its very shape, moreover—a series of questions and answers—betrays a visibly fluctuating movement in the quest for certainty laid down by its theme. It is a poem which may be taken as one of the most lucid representations of the central situation implicit in the last tragic poems:[1]

> All that I have said and done
> Now that I am old and ill
> Turns into a question till

[1] Another poem, 'Phases of the Moon', written as early as 1918, ostensibly to serve as a specific illustration of how the 'system' worked (an illustration of a kind which Yeats said he would never make again), can also be taken as an early attempt to wrest an answer from the mocking question of 'The Man and the Echo'. Like the later poem, it is a scourge upon the poet. In 'Phases of the Moon' two creatures of Yeats's romantic imagination stand below the lighted tower of the labouring poet and mock him. Because they are made objective personae who embody specified values, they have the somewhat puzzling effect of making the poet seem to endorse them, while, at the same time, one can detect his regret that he has not trusted his own insight. Later, when Yeats had assimilated the 'system' so that it was no longer a system, he was able to use its concepts with great spontaneity and freedom. Perhaps this only means that he cared less for it.

'Turns into a question till'—that is the spiritual burden of these poems. But the questions remain unanswered, and 'The Man and the Echo' is merely the superb statement of the paradox. 'The Gyres' must therefore be considered a more ambitious venture, and its centrality to the last poems derives not only from the field it itself inhabits, but also from the attempt it makes to reconcile the bitter opposites left unresolved by 'The Man and the Echo'.[1]

Yeats wrote this poem in July 1939, under an apprehension of death. It is one, which Dr. Jeffares soundly reminds us, 'must be read aloud for its exquisite verbal music to be valued'. As I have said, it is one of the least obscure of the last poems, and, because there is available an early version of July 1938 which Yeats, as was his habit then, sent to Dorothy Wellesley, we can read it against the published version. We can get from such a comparison a good understanding of his technical practice in the great days at the end.

Like many of Yeats's poems written in that last decade, 'The Man and the Echo' is dominated by images of rock, stone, caverns and mysterious voices which shout into the deep night of the self. It employs the convention of 'Ego Dominus Tuus', written twenty years before, in which two speakers, Hic and Ille (or, as a Dublin wag put it, Hic and Willie), are the two polar aspects of the self, made more concrete in the

[1] It is possible that the idea of a 'key' poem or 'key' poems, as unlocking problems inhering in a group of poems, might prove as useful to the critic, if judiciously invoked, as that of 'key' words in a single poem.

later poem as 'Man' and 'Echo'. The outward dialogue frame of both poems is an organic reflection of the inner dichotomy. In 'The Man and the Echo', the Man confronts himself at night (night, the model of death) and shouts a secret to the stone (the unyielding face of the universe which will not give up its mystery; also the calcified parts of the self which guard a similar secret life).

In the early version the assertion that all the Man has done has turned into a question is put even more brutally: he 'seems to have done but harm . . .'. The revision makes for a sharper weighing; the evil is not so heavily drawn. It is for this reason that the dramatic tension between the two aspects of the self is better-sustained. In the unpublished version the last lines of stanza one read:

> I say that I have done some good
> As well as evil, but in this mood
> I see but evil until I
> Sleepless would lie down and die.

Yeats eliminates the first and second lines and makes the third more tragic in the damning self-judgment pointed to by the accented 'all' in the closing lines:

> And all seems evil until I
> Sleepless would lie down and die.

The significant changes in stanza two show up his surprisingly prosy diction when first drafting a poem.[1] They are especially illustrative of Yeats's unfailing

[1] Louis MacNeice has said that Yeats often first wrote a prose statement of a projected poem.

touchstone in revision: Does the revision increase the effect of spoken language? Thus, for the early

> And he unless his mind is sure
> That its vision of life is true

where the hippety-hop banality of the last line is unrelieved by a single strong word, Yeats wrote:

> And till his intellect grows sure
> That all's arranged in one clear view

The substitution of a positive for a negative construction in line one, the substitution of an active verb 'grows', and a phonetically distinctive one 'is arranged' for the simple copulative 'is' of both lines; the more exact noun 'intellect', which stresses the ordering, analytic qualities of 'mind', a vaguer entity; the musical intensity of 'clear view', suggesting a clairvoyance which pierces almost physically, rather than the abstract and passive approbation of 'is true'—all these changes show Yeats employing his most incisive critical perceptions.

Perhaps the most strengthening change is from:

> Then he, being satisfied, blots all
> Human existence from his sight.

to:

> And, all work done, dismisses all
> And sinks at last into the night.

The repetition of 'all' at the beginning and end of the first line stamps a finality upon it missing from the earlier version. The clumsy and passive participial construction 'being satisfied' is discarded for the less smug, more fluent, and more absolute 'All work done'. 'Dismisses', for 'blots', is a gain in precision and purposiveness, as if the will had a more exact control over conduct. The 'all' which replaces 'Human existence' is equally abstract but less prosy, and, because even less specific than the former, embraces a greater mystery.

When in the last stanza the Man addresses Echo as 'O Rocky Voice' (originally, 'O rocky void') we are reminded of 'The Gyres' not only, as I have remarked, because of the likeness of this appellation to 'Old Rocky Face' but also because Echo is asked a question which is answered in terms almost identical with the theme of 'The Gyres'. The question is here put: 'Shall we in that great night rejoice?' In 'The Gyres', it will be remembered, the answer is:

> ... Out of cavern comes a voice
> And all it knows is that one word 'Rejoice!'

while in 'The Man and the Echo', the protagonist reproaches his self for even raising the question:

> But hush! for I have lost the theme
> Its joy or night seem but a dream;

Now death (denial) and rejoicing (acceptance) seem equally a matter of appearance. It is important to note that this couplet was added to the early version. The addition complicates the dialogue structure, producing a kind of interior monologue within the one aspect of self signified by 'Man'.

But, at the last, an end is put to the destructive ambivalence of such introspection. Life, in the form of simple energies impinges upon the thinker's consciousness and 'distracts' him from the 'pit' of negation. Now the Man and his Echo merge:

> Up there some hawk or owl has struck
> Dropping out of sky or rock
> A stricken rabbit is crying out,
> And its cry distracts my thought.

It is *life* which triumphs, even if momentarily, and on the brink of the grave. And characteristically, it is a 'stricken' rabbit that Yeats sees as the agency of enough life to distract him from death. The creativity of suffering, the claims of suffering upon 'life', had never been put by Yeats with such a tender pity. The rabbit's cry can be taken, I am willing to hazard, as the answer to the pit, to negation, and to the rocky voice of Echo. It evokes by a brief and modest image the flowing continuity of all vital experience, which, in one form or another Yeats tried to find, and, trying, *found* as the answer to his perplexities. While it is true, as Mr. Ure has said of the last poems that 'A divided mind is at the heart of this poetry', it is also true that at times the divisions fuse into the objective resolution of a given poem. 'The Man and the Echo' provides one of the most memorable of these occasions.

GROUP FOUR

1. THE THREE BUSHES

2. THE LADY'S FIRST SONG

3. THE LADY'S SECOND SONG

4. THE LADY'S THIRD SONG

5. THE LOVER'S SONG

6. THE CHAMBERMAID'S FIRST SONG

7. THE CHAMBERMAID'S SECOND SONG

THE THREE BUSHES

*(An incident from the 'Historia mei Temporis' of
the Abbe Michel de Bourdeille)*

Said lady once to lover,
'None can reply upon
A love that lacks its proper food;
And if your love were gone
How could you sing those songs of love?
I should be blamed, young man.'
    O my dear, O my dear.

'Have no lit candles in your room,'
That lovely lady said,
'That I at midnight by the clock
May creep into your bed,
For if I saw myself creep in
I think I should drop dead.'
    O my dear, O my dear.

'I love a man in secret,
Dear chambermaid,' said she
'I know that I must drop down dead
If he stop loving me,
Yet what could I but drop down dead
If I lost my chastity?'
    O my dear, O my dear.

123

'So you must lie beside him
And let me think me there,
And maybe we are all the same
Where no candles are,
And maybe we are all the same,
That strip the body bare.'
O my dear, O my dear.

But no dogs barked, and midnights chimed,
And through the chime she'd say,
'That was a lucky thought of mine,
My lover looked so gay';
But heaved a sigh if the chambermaid
Looked half asleep all day.
O my dear, O my dear.

'No, not another song,' said he,
'Because my lady came
A year ago for the first time
At midnight to my room,
And I must lie between the sheets
When the clock begins to chime.'
O my dear, O my dear.

'A laughing, crying, sacred song,
A leching song,' they said,
Did ever men hear such a song?
No, but that day they did.
Did ever man ride such a race?
No, not until he rode.
O my dear, O my dear.

But when his horse had put its hoof
Into a rabbit-hole
He dropped upon his head and died.
His lady saw it all
And dropped and died thereon, for she
   Loved him with her soul.
     O my dear, O my dear.

The chambermaid lived long, and took
Their graves into her charge,
And there two bushes planted
That when they had grown large
Seemed sprung from but a single root
So did their roses merge.
     O my dear, O my dear.

When she was old and dying,
The priest came where she was;
She made a full confession.
Long looked he in her face,
And O he was a good man
And understood her case.
     O my dear, O my dear.

He bade them take and bury her
Beside her lady's man,
And set a rose tree on her grave,
And now none living can,
When they have plucked a rose there,
Know where its roots began.
     O my dear, O my dear.

THE LADY'S FIRST SONG

I turn round
Like a dumb beast in a show,
Neither know what I am
Nor where I go,
My language beaten
Into one name;
I am in love
And that is my shame.
What hurts the soul
My soul adores,
No better than a beast
Upon all fours.

THE LADY'S SECOND SONG

What sort of man is coming
To lie between your feet?
What matter, we are but women.
Wash; make your body sweet;
I have cupboards of dried fragrance,
I can strew the sheet.
        The Lord have mercy upon us.

He shall love my soul as though
Body were not all,
He shall love your body
Untroubled by the soul,

Love cram love's two divisions
Yet keep his substance whole.
> *The Lord have mercy upon us.*

Soul must learn a love that is
Proper to my breast,
Limbs a love in common
With every noble beast.
If soul may look and body touch,
Which is the more blest?
> *The Lord have mercy upon us.*

THE LADY'S THIRD SONG

When you and my true lover meet
And he plays tunes between your feet,
Speak no evil of the soul,
Nor think that body is the whole,
For I that am his daylight lady
Know worse evil of the body;
But in honour split his love
Till either neither have enough,
That I may hear if we should kiss
A contrapuntal serpent hiss,
You, should hand explore a thigh,
All the labouring heavens sigh.

THE LOVER'S SONG

Bird sighs for the air,
Thought for I know not where,
For the womb the seed sighs.
Now sinks the same rest
On mind, on nest,
On straining thighs.

THE CHAMBERMAID'S FIRST SONG

How came this ranger
Now sunk in rest,
Stranger with stranger,
On my cold breast?
What's left to sigh for,
Strange night has come;
God's love has hidden him
Out of all harm,
Pleasure has made him
Weak as a worm.

THE CHAMBERMAID'S SECOND SONG

From pleasure of the bed,
Dull as a worm,
His rod and its butting head
Limp as a worm,
His spirit that has fled
Blind as a worm.

I

THE THREE BUSHES

By the above heading I refer to the poem of that name and the six following 'Songs' which comprise what is really a unified song-sequence. There has been a singular silence observed regarding these poems by Yeats's recent biographers. I am unable to discover a single reference to them in either Dr. Jeffares's or Mr. Ellman's books. Yet Yeats himself, as I have mentioned elsewhere, attached such importance to them that he wished the sequence in the small section he had allowed for his own work in the *Oxford Book of Modern Verse*. One is led to wonder whether the critical silence is one of embarrassment for the openly sexual themes and imagery of these poems. It is as if it were felt that they were an awkward mistake on the part of the old poet, who for every other poem of the same period is accorded superlatives. One can only come to the conclusion that the challenge of the sexual theme, when it is not tricked out in remote or exotic images, is intimidating for the critic to handle, even when the same critic devotes a questionable emphasis to the 'events' of Yeats's own sexual experience which are, anyhow, for the most part, unverifiable.

But perhaps this is a misleading introduction to what are surely among the strangest love poems ever written, and which, however odd, grotesque or difficult to accept, we cannot dismiss as the temporary aberrations of an artist who, concurrently with them, was composing other works of genius. Yeats himself, no mean judge of his own work, however poor a judge of others, thought 'The Three Bushes' a 'masterpiece'.[1] His correspondence with Dorothy Wellesley during the period of its composition has many illuminating references to it. There is one early version, and in one case three versions, for each of the seven poems, thus making the sequence an instructive source for the analysis of the final technical repertoire at Yeats's command.

The sequence shows Yeats trying to explore the sexual paradox within the limits of a dramatic fable even narrower than those of his plays, and thus producing a greater intensity in the poetry. By keeping to a dramatic fiction, he was freed to employ the three separate voices of the Lady, the Chambermaid and the Lover in the 'Songs' and the fourth choric voice of a narrator. It is he who utters the pitying refrain: 'O my dear, O my dear.'[2] The greater lyrical objectivity

[1] *Letters to Dorothy Wellesley*, 2 July 1936. But, it should be added, Yeats said this of many poems of this period.

[2] The function of the refrain has been admirably outlined by Mr. MacNeice who notices a change in intention from about 1920 on, pointing out that in many of the later songs the refrain is the focal point of the poem. In the present study, the refrain in 'The Wild Old Wicked Man' and the first poem of 'The Three Bushes' partially illustrate this tendency. For while I should not call '*Daybreak and a candle end*', or '*O my dear, O my dear*', the focal points of these poems, they do provide objective statements made by the omniscient narrating voice, and thus carry great authority in determining the total meaning of the poem.

afforded by such dramatization was strengthened by the traditional ballad frame of the introductory poem. That Yeats wished, with the same naughty wilfulness with which he had hoaxed the introduction to the 1926 edition of *A Vision*, to persuade the reader that this was a true incident is clear. In a note to Dorothy Wellesley on 15th November 1936 he says: 'I am describing "The Three Bushes" as "founded" upon an incident from the "Historia nei Temporis" of the Abbé Michel de Bourdelie.' The spelling of the Abbé's name, as the reader will note, was no doubt fixed up by some kind friend for the printed version. But whether Bourdelie, or Bourdeille, the pun on *bordel* is obvious. When such a cognomen is fastened upon an Abbé, Yeats's familiar design in this period of foisting the secular upon the holy is intimated. But how the poem accomplishes a similar fusion—and not without some incidental ribaldry—is what I am most concerned to examine.

The first mention of the poems comes in a letter of July 1936, which suggests Yeats has been at the project for a time: 'I now like my long ballad of "The Three Bushes" again. I have written two other poems on the same theme . . . I think them among my best things.' That he later saw the sequence as a single unit of poetic expressions and as an essentially dramatic one is made clear in a letter to Dorothy Wellesley on 20th November of the same year. Speaking of 'The Lady's First Song', he writes: 'It is supposed to be spoken by the Lady before her two poems addressed to the Chamber-

maid. . . . It is not in itself very good but it will heighten
the drama.' Yeats's decision to allow a less intense passage to stand because it contributes to the total intention of the dramatic action is cognate with the principle
earlier discussed of relying on the dull words in a poem
to set off the radiance of the vivid ones, while yet con-
tributing to the line of the argument.[1]

The narrative line of the sequence is simple: a Lady
who loves a poet, and wisely recognizes that love needs
to be fed, at the same time wishes to preserve her
chastity. She asks her chambermaid to lie with her lover
in her stead: 'And maybe we are all the same that strip
the body bare.' She is pleased with herself for her
strategy but nevertheless has faint regrets when the
chambermaid 'looked half asleep all day'. Later on, the
lover, out drinking, turns down the offer of another
song and says he must return to the bed where his lady
a year ago first came to him. On his way back to the
rendezvous, his horse puts its hoof in a rabbit-hole and
the man is killed. His lady, seeing the accident, herself
drops dead. The chambermaid takes their two graves
in charge and plants two bushes which grow as if
'sprung from but a single root'. When she is old and
dying, she confesses and the priest ('O he was a good
man/And understood her case) bids she be buried by
her lady's man with a rose tree on her grave. Now none

---

[1]. Eliot, a far more systematic critic of poetry, but one who,
I think, learned a great deal from Yeats, has made an interesting
amplification of this principle in *The Music of Poetry* where he
argues that it is necessary in constructing the long poem to
bridge the highly concentrated sections with more prosaic passages.

can tell where the roots of any rose there began, so entwined are the three bushes.

The following six lyrics, all short, purport to be spoken by the Lady (three); by the Lover (one, and significantly, the paltriest) and by the Chambermaid (two), whose last song ends the sequence. The narrative technique is that of the flashback, for the three personae have already been disposed of in the introductory poem. But in the songs the psychological facets of their rôles in the drama are explored by each in turn. 'The Lady's First Song' tells of her 'shame' because she is in love and 'No better than a beast/Upon all fours'. It describes her ambivalence toward the sexual union she appears to shun and shows the degradation she attaches to what she craves. 'The Lady's Second Song' (the early version is called 'The Lady to her Chambermaid') advises the maid to prepare herself for the Lover, who will love the maid's body but love the Lady's soul. It is considerably more complex in tone than her first song, and closes with a paradox:

If soul may look and body touch
Which is the more blest?

'The Lady's Third Song' is even more subtle in diction and meaning. It presents a quite involved rationale of the Lady's stratagem which puts her motives for not sleeping with her lover in a more generous light. She says she wishes her maid to share with her the aspect of love which bodily union does not touch, just as she participates vicariously in the bodily union which her lover enjoys with the maid.

133

'The Lover's Song', simplest of all, has the least 'colour'. The Lover is almost a blind force seeking to discharge its burden of necessity in much the same instinctual way that 'Bird sighs for the air'. The mind is pacified by being rid of the burden imposed on it by the body.

The Chambermaid's songs (the ones which cause readers the most embarrassment; they offended Dorothy Wellesley, too) are strange, bold descriptions of sexual intercourse and its aftermath. The metre of both short lyrics is that of a lullaby; the tone infinitely tender, even maternal:

> God's love has hidden him
> Out of all harm.

The second song of the maid, which we at first may take as a low-pitched one of *dégoût d'amour* is, in reality, an elegy sung for the departed Lover. In it we see the Chambermaid in a separate aspect of her rôle, *after* the deception, when her chagrin at the narrowness of her experience with her lady's man overcomes her ('His spirit that has fled/Blind as a worm'). In tone, it is an intensification of the mood of her first song.[1]

The narrative thus outlined, we are faced with a question: Is there a split in the 'story' summarized by the objective introductory poem, and the 'story' as revealed by the individual characters who later speak

[1] Originally, and this is a clue to Yeats's intention, the Chambermaid's first song was called 'The Chambermaid's prayer before Dawn', and the second song, 'The Chambermaid's song after his death'. Letter to Dorothy Wellesley of 15 November 1936.

their part in it? We know that the end of the total story is positive and happy: all three lovers are united in death by the symbolic merging of the bushes into a single organism. The incompleteness of their relationships in life are seen to supplement one another in the longer view. Body and soul, as the lady suspected, but could not risk proving, are, in the end, one. Why, then, with a pretty and almost 'poetical' ending to his opening ballad, does Yeats allow the little drama to trail off in the let-down cadences of the Chambermaid's second song?

While I am not sure that I have the answer to this, I am equally sure that the difficulty felt is not merely rhetorical. I suggest a musical analogy as a possible way out: 'The Three Bushes' is somewhat like the overture of an opera which presents the 'story' by means of a recapitulation of the main themes; the little songs are the individual arias and, as such, are both an elucidation and an enrichment of the main plot. But, to go further than this, or to imagine that this analogy was a purpose upon which Yeats built is not possible. I have tried to read the sequence in reverse; that is, all the songs first and then 'The Three Bushes', as exposition and summing-up, but this leaves the songs unanchored in a plot and thus uncertain in direction until the very last lines. The actual arrangement, quite obviously, has its drawbacks or this issue should not have arisen: we are given the resolution at the beginning, and left with a brutal reduction of sexuality at the end. Is this what Yeats wanted to leave as the final impression of the fable? Or was he simply mistaken in assuming that the reader's memory would hold the attractive image of 'The Three Bushes' before him in the realization that the Chambermaid's elegiac remorse is a flashback to the time before she and the others are seen from an Olympian vantage in their less temporal connection.

There is evidence that the last Chambermaid poem troubled Yeats, for there are two early versions included in the letters to Dorothy Wellesley. The first of these versions is especially useful, for Yeats (as almost always in early versions) is remarkably explicit about his 'theme'. It reads:

> Joy laid him on my bed
> Weak as a worm,
> His rod, that rose up unfed
> Limp as a worm,
> A shadow has gone to the dead
> Thin as a worm
> Where can his spirit have fled
> Bare as a worm.

The most significant feature is the first line. It describes in abstract terms and less vigorously the event which, in the published version, is narrowed down to a specific act in a specific context. The specific act is seen generically, the definite article before 'bed' effecting a generic dimension. Thus, only one kind of pleasure is credited with this effect. The gain is one in precision of meaning. The first assertion was so inclusive as to be imprecise. That Yeats was dissatisfied with the line is clear for in the second version written out in a letter

136

five days later (20th November 1936) it becomes 'Joy let him upon my bed'. Other changes are made, in partial explanation of which Yeats writes: '. . . the second line wrongly expressed in the version I sent you two days ago "unfed" being clearly the reverse of true.' The line now reads (as in the printed version): 'His rod and its butting head', and the gain in phonetic power, as well as the autonomy conferred upon the phallus by the detail of the 'butting head', dramatizes in kinetic terms exactly that instinctual and mysterious dynamism in the sexual act which Yeats sees as a spiritual principle animating the universe. It is only in this light that the last two lines of the poem have any meaning.

It is important, in this connection, to note that the syntax has been changed from interrogative to declarative form. The prevalence of questions in the later poetry of Yeats is a recurring sign that tells us something about the quality of his explorations; among other things, by preserving the *form* of his interest—an ever-widening quest—we are given the sense of our own involvement in a similar search. Thus, when Yeats changes 'Where can his spirit have fled?' in version one to 'His spirit that has fled' in versions two and three, his intention is visibly didactic: he is emphasizing the evanescence of the *possession* by spirit, or even more ambiguously, *a* spirit, which transpires in the sexual act. The possessive 'His' before 'spirit' is deliberately unanchored. It is man's spirit, and also the spirit of the phallus, both being fused in that 'Unity of Being' effected by the sexual agency. 'Blind as a worm' pre-

137

sents a similar double-ness of implication: it is the phallus 'blind', that is, unpurposive, not directed to its function. It is equally the dead man 'blind', that is, no longer possessed by the directing instinctual power; and, in the end, it is the power, itself 'blind', because, like a worm, a primary, instinctual form of energy.

I shall continue to work backward in looking at the revisions for in this way we shall get the summing-up of 'The Three Bushes' last. In 'The Chambermaid's First Song', a first version of which we find in the letter of 15th November, the most significant differences from the published version fall in the second half of the poem. After the line 'What's left to sigh for', Yeats has:

> Now all are the same?
> What would he die for
> Before night came?

It will be seen that, as in 'The Chambermaid's Second Song', the revision is again away from a too explicit statement of the theme. The rather commonplace observation that in sexual experience everyone is the same is deleted, leaving the second version a line shorter. The question of the two lines following (really a disguised assertion stating, by indirection, that the values by which the lover's daylight life are measured differ from those of his night) is also deleted. Instead, in the one fine line, more richly and musically integrated with the total sound-meaning pattern of the poem,

> Strange night has come

Yeats telescopes the deleted three. The 'night' is night; it is also the mysterious death-like resolution of the antagonistic principles of experience which Yeats said were resolved, if anywhere, in the marriage-bed. 'Strange', an adjective, bears out the normative 'Stranger with stranger' in line three, and, because it benefits from its earlier use, it becomes highly charged. Night is 'strange', mysterious, rich.

'The Lover's Song', as I have hinted, is of all the least personal and least dramatic. Its quiet lyricism suggests an almost passive acceptance by the Lover of his rôle in the instinctual scheme. The detail is that of the natural scene: a few representative features (bird, nest, seed) are made co-evalent with some representative details in the sexual nexus. It is one of the few poems about sex in which Yeats is not seeking to objectify his own sexual interest as a man. Instead, there is such an easy identification of the rôle of the dramatic speaker with that of the Lover that the poet's own motive is completely absorbed into the almost anonymous lyricism.

That this should happen in a sequence which Yeats conceived in a primarily dramatic dimension is significant. The Lover's attitude is the most perfectly 'philosophic' in temper; he is hardly a person at all, except in so far as he is able to take himself as the sign of a more universal force. It is 'rest' that bird, thighs, and mind alike seek, not, to use the chambermaid's phrase, 'pleasure of the bed'. The lover, unlike the two women actors of the drama, is completely unspeculative and without vacillation. It is, ironically, really the two women who decide his fate for him.[1] Reversing the conventional weighting, *they* are the agents; he, the instrument. The fact that there is no early version for this little lyric included in Yeats's letter does not, of course, mean that there was none, but it does suggest that he felt no insecurity about its rightness. It represents, one senses, the most fully adult understanding of the teleology of the male sexual rôle which Yeats anywhere achieved. It is thoroughly 'unromantic'.

Still working backward, the Lady's second and third songs must be considered together. Originally, they were one. 'The Lady's Third Song' in the version sent to Dorothy Wellesley on 15th July was part two of the second song. After considerable alteration, Yeats broke it off and set it up as a separate entity. Both songs are addressed to the Chambermaid by the Lady, but it will be observed that the diction of the third song represents a slight heightening in the element of 'metaphysicality' (roughly, language suited to the rendering of ambiguity and paradox). It was fitting, therefore, to separate it from the second song and thus to preserve its character as song. The refrain, '*The Lord have mercy*

[1] Even the circumstances of the Lover's death—his horse puts his foot in a rabbit hole—underlines the womb-tomb symbolism of the actual relationship between him and the two women. This would seem to reflect the notion put forward in *A Vision* and which Yeats cautiously credits to his 'instructors' that 'When my instructors see woman as man's goal and limit, rather than as mother, they symbolize her as *Mask* and *Body of Fate*, object of desire and object of thought, the one a perpetual rediscovery of what the other destroys . . . and they set this double opposition in perpetual opposition to *Will* and *Creative Mind*'.

upon us' gives a ritual air, as well as slyly commenting on the secular content.

The original unit was written in unrhymed couplets, set off from one another. Now, the second song is integrated into three stanzas, sestets unified by an identical refrain. The second part, now the third song, is the most heavily revised, being, in fact, almost entirely rewritten. This redirection of linguistic means reflects a shift in Yeats's intention when he came to this half of the song. The inevitably right gesture was to see it as an independent, if sequential, unit in the Lady's experience. And Yeats made it.

I shall comment only on the most pointed revisions. For lines five and six, we have:

> I must that am his daylight lady
> Outrageously abuse the body;

What Yeats has done is consistent with his usual practice. He has toned down the passage by making it less imperative in syntax and less violent in language. To substitute 'Know worse evil of the body' for 'Outrageously abuse the body' is to produce a greater obliquity. The assertion that by denying herself to her lover she is really abusing her body is nevertheless still the denotative content of the line. But the attendant horror of such self-knowledge is better evoked by the less specific 'Know worse evil of the body'. The following revision is even more valuable. For the original

> Swear that he shall never stray
> From either neither night and day

Yeats wrote:

> But in honour split his love
> Till either neither have enough.

How right he is, both in terms of the archaic setting
and the strange compact that they have made between
them, that the Lady should invoke 'honour' in her
curiously searching but humble request! The language
is apt for this end: the really dramatic word 'split'
polarizes around it the terms that the split experience
of love represents for the two women. That this contributes to the basic paradox of the poem is obvious,
but that it facilitates the poem's movement to its crisis
in the next four lines is less evident. Yet it is the crucial
word 'split' that prepares us to accept:

> That I may hear if we should kiss
> A contrapuntal serpent hiss,
> You, should hand explore a thigh,
> All the labouring heavens sigh.

Yeats never used language more intellectually, and,
at the same time, more lyrically than in this little song.
To say it reminds one of Donne is not to explain it,
but to place it. The refinement of a phrase like 'contrapuntal serpent hiss' is not only successful for the complexity of the whole sexual nexus—act and the valuation
of act—which it denotes, but also for the connection
it establishes with the daring metaphor of the start: the
Lover as a musician playing tunes on the body of the
loved one. There is an elegance in the poem's verbal
music, a music that can be properly got only by read-

ing aloud. It is, moreover, a music all the more appropriate for its delicacy of tonal effects (note the lovely half-rhyme of 'lady' and 'body') because of the ambiguity of the 'ideas' involved.

In the 'Lady's Second Song' she had sketched the horns of the moral dilemma in which she found herself:

> Soul must learn a love that is
> Proper to my breast,
> Limbs a love in common
> With every noble beast.
> If soul may look and body touch
> Which is the more blest?
> *The Lord have mercy upon us.*

But in the third song she offers an answer which is not so much a slipping between the horns as an acceptance of the complementary opposition they represent. It is reasonable to suppose that Yeats meant this as an answer not merely to the Lady's or the Chambermaid's cut-off experience of love, but also as an answer to those who dichotomize love into the contraries of bodily love and spiritual love. Here, as in Donne, the contraries are seen to co-exist and to fecundate one another. In this connection, the striking antithesis of 'kiss' and 'hiss' must be recognized as more than a felicitous rhyme, for it dramatizes, in sensuous terms, exactly that polarity which the last lines successfully integrate. (The serpent symbol, it should be added, also connects with the 'blind worm' in the Chambermaid's song. 'Serpent' and 'worm' are two aspects of

143

an identical force.) But the integration I speak of represents a development in the Lady's own morality. In her first song, a song which, as I have said, Yeats did not much care for, she is capable only of guilt and shame for that which love makes her share with a 'dumb beast'. She sees no more than a cleavage between sense and soul. It is only later that her moral sense deepens to a perception of the 'contrapuntal' harmonies to be wrested from such opposites.

Now that we have come full circle, we can more fully see 'The Three Bushes' as introduction, exposition and summing-up of the sequence. Let us look at the heavily revised first stanza which Yeats had originally given to Dorothy Wellesley in a letter of 15th November:

> 'Man's love that lacks its proper food
> None can rely upon
> And could you sing no more of love
> Your genius would be gone
> And could that happen what were you
> But a starving man.'
> *O my dear, O my dear.*

What has happened between this and the version we know is that the dramatic tension has been heightened. The obviously biographical references to genius and its requirements are suppressed,[1] and the poem more

[1] As a young man, Yeats confesses in the *Autobiographies*: 'I took great pleasure in certain allusions to the singer's life one finds in old romances and ballads and thought his presence there the more poignant because we discover it half-lost.' But he never truly reconciled this with his desire 'to create once more an art where the artist's handiwork would hide as under those half-anonymous chisels'.

clearly sets its theme as the conflict *within* love, rather than the conflict between love and art, which the first version superfluously introduces. This removal from the area of Yeats's personal motive is good for the poem, although he wrote other good poems dedicated to it. The removal lends the subject aesthetic distance and makes possible the neatly-etched fable. But perhaps this is putting the cart before the horse although, in poetic composition, we should not wish to have the horse before the cart either.

The difference between the two versions can be better accounted for if we allow that the actual work on the poem clarified for Yeats the direction in which he wished it to go. Out of this draft of the first stanza of the poem, which later precipitated the whole sequence, we can reconstruct the nearness of the theme to his own conflicts. The increased objectivity of the revised stanza is a token of his later intention for the sequence. He wishes to maintain the free intellectual scrutiny of 'love' which the fiction of the three actors allows. For, while the speakers represent different facets of the problem, they all contribute to one organic vision of the meaning of 'love'. The last stanza of 'The Three Bushes' is the symbolic resolution of the temporal conflicts of the songs into an integrated moral statement. And the deliberate quiet of these lines is the drawing of the curtain upon the radiant constellation of that sexual universe which so attracted Yeats to the very end.

CONCLUSION

Whatever effect of unity Yeats secured in the last poems was achieved at the cost of ignoring the many great contributions made by others to the intellectual life of his times. The limitation which Yeats never quite grasped is that the concept of 'Unity' or homogeneity in a culture, like the ideal of homogeneity in a race, can only be achieved at the price of a ruthless genocide of ideas. The 'Unity' thus attained is never that, as we can see from Yeats's quite tawdry 'system' in *A Vision*, but rather an intensely perceived segment of the arc of possible human richness. When such a segment is taken for a whole, it may prove useful to the one who sets it up, or to his disciples. But that such wilful and exclusive 'ordering' can give direction to others is doubtful.[1]

And, even for Yeats, if we weigh the testimony of the last poems properly, the 'system' at the close failed him. But perhaps it is this very failure we should thank for their high turbulence. For they stand as the live 'monuments of unageing intellect'; their desperate gallantry represents the best order Yeats could construct from

[1] Among the critics who make, to my mind, absurd claims for the value of Yeats's 'ideas' is Mr. Graham Hough, who, in his recent study, *The Last Romantics*, holds that Yeats's world-view is more inclusive than Catholicism.

147

the sea of disorder by which he felt himself threatened.
Each poem thus carries upon it the sign of its struggle;
each represents a lasting tribute wrested from 'That
dolphin-torn, that gong-tormented sea'.

INDEX

'Acres of Grass, An,' *quoted in full*, 43; 45–54

'All Soul's Night,' 96 fn.

'Among Schoolchildren,' 20

Anthology, The, 64

Aquinas, St. Thomas, 97

Arnold, Matthew, 52, 111

Autobiographies, 24, 67, 98, 144 fn.

BBC (British Broadcasting Corporation), 24

Blake, William, 14 fn., 15, 16, 47; *Visions of the Daughters of Albion*, 68

Blavatsky, Madame, 106

Bronowski, Dr. J., 15–17; *The Poet's Defence*, 16 fn.

'Bronze Head, A,' *quoted in full*, 77–8; 79–87

Brooks, Cleanth, 20

Buddha, 60, 72, 73

'Byzantium,' 16, 84, 96 fn.

Campbell, Lawrence, 79

'Chambermaid's First Song, The,' *quoted in full*, 128; 138

'Chambermaid's Second Song, The,' *quoted in full*, 128; 138

'Coat, A,' 103 fn.

Cuchalain, 62; 64, 73

'Curse of Cromwell, The,' 40

Dante, 100

'Demon and Beast,' 96 fn.

Donne, John, 51, 52–3, 142, 143

Dramatis Personae, 52

Dulac, Edmund, 24

Easter Rebellion, 63

'Ego Dominus Tuus,' 100, 116

Eliot, T. S., 14–15, 26, 108–9, 132; *The Wasteland*, 73 fn.; *The Music of Poetry*, 132 fn.

Ellman, Richard, 17, 18, 93, 129

Emerson, Ralph W., 70

Four Quartets, 14

'Four Years,' 60

'Full Moon in March, A,' 105 fn.

'Geneological Tree of Revolution,' 13

Golden Nightingale, The, 19–20

Gonne, Maud, 61, 62, 63, 67, 75, 79, 82–4, 86–7

'Gyres, The,' 19, 64 fn., *quoted in full*, 91; 93–111, 115, 116, 119

Hamilton, G. Restrevor, *The Tell-Tale Article*, 50–1; 52

Hegel, G. W. F., 13
Hone, Joseph, 17; *W. B. Yeats,
1865–1939*, 17
Hough, Graham, *The Last Romantics*, 147
Hügel, F. von, *The Mystical Element of Religion*, 104

Jeffares, Dr. A. Norman, 13, 17, 21, 23, 33, 46, 47, 79, 84 fn., 94, 95, 101, 105, 129
Joyce, James, *Ulysses, Finnigans Wake*, 73 fn.

Kant, Immanuel, 13
Kierkegaard, 104 fn.

'Lady's First Song, 'The,' *quoted in full*, 126; 131, 133
'Lady's Second Song, The,' *quoted in full*, 126–7; 133, 143
'Lady's Third Song, The,' *quoted in full*, 127; 135, 140
'Lady to Her Chambermaid, The,' 133
'Lake Isle of Innisfree, The,' 36, 48
Last Poems, 51, 59, 93, 101, 102
Letters to Dorothy Wellesley, 130 fn.
'Long-Legged Fly,' 80 fn.
'Lover's Song, The,' *quoted in full*, 128; 134, 139

MacNeice, Louis, 45, 71 fn., 117 fn., 130 fn.
McTaggart, John, *Studies in Hegelian Cosmology*, 81–2

'Man and the Echo, The,' 100, *quoted in full*, 113–4; 115–9
Marx, Karl, 13
'Matrix,' 22
Morris, William, 60, 62

Nicholas of Cusa, 13
Nietzsche, *The Dawn of Day*, 46
Nineteenth Century, The, 110 fn.

On the Boiler, 70 fn.
'Only Jealousy of Emer, The,' 86
Owen, Wilfred, 34
Oxford Book of Modern Verse, 21, 34,

Pelham, Lady Elizabeth, 33 fn.
Petrie, Flinders, *The Revolution of Civilizations*, 104
'Phases of the Moon,' 107 fn., 115 fn.
Pound, Ezra, 48, 109; *Cantos*, 73 fn.
Pythagoras, 66–73

Rabelais, François, 46
Rajan, Dr. B., 'W. B. Yeats and the Unity of Being,' 110
Responsibilities, 15, 51
Riding, Laura, 39

'Second Coming, The,' 64, 84, 93, 94 fn., 96
Shakespear, Mrs., 96
Shakespeare, William, 85
Shelley, Percy Bysshe, 94, 99, 100–1

150

'Shepherd and Goatherd,' 96 fn.

Sparrow, John, 26

'Statues, The,' *quoted in full,* 57–8; 59–75, 105 fn.

Stauffer, Donald, 18–20, 93, 94 fn.

Steinach, 21

Strong, Mrs. Eugénie, *Apotheosis and After-Life,* 96

Swedenborg, Emmanuel, 97

Swinburne, Algernon C., 15

Thompson, Francis, 94–5

'Those Images,' 101

'Three Bushes, The,' 21, 22, 23, 34; *quoted in full,* 123–5; 129–45

Titian, 60

'Tower, The,' 93

Tragic Generation, The, 109

Trembling of the Veil, The, 48, 98

Ure, Peter, *Towards a Mythology: Studies in the Poetry of W. B. Yeats,* 63; 86, 120

Vico, 13

Vision, A, 17, 24, 26, 26 fn., 36, 46, 59, 65, 67, 79, 83 fn., 84, 93, 94, 95, 96, 97, 103, 107 fn., 131, 140 fn., 147

Watts, George Frederick, 60

Wellesley, Dorothy (Lady Gerald), 22, 23, 34, 36, 39, 40, 51, 62, 68, 97, 100, 116, 130, 131, 133, 136, 140, 144

'What Then?' 40

'Wild Old Wicked Man, The,' *quoted in full,* 29; 33–41, 45, 130 fn.

Yeats, Mrs. W. B., 21

Yeats, W. B.: Man and Poet, 13 fn.

Yeats, The Man and The Masks, 17